On the Mother Lagoon

Fly Fishing and the Spiritual Journey

Kathy Sparrow

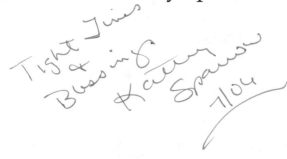

Wish Publishing
Terre Haute, Indiana
www.wishpublishing.com

LCCN: 2002109916

Editorial assistance provided by Natalie Chambers
Proofread by Ken Samelson
Cover designed by Phil Velikan
Cover photography by Scott Sparrow
Interior photography by Scott Sparrow

Printed in the United States of America
10 9 8 7 6 5 4 3 2 1

Published in the United States by
Wish Publishing
P.O. Box 10337
Terre Haute, IN 47801, USA
www.wishpublishing.com

Distributed in the United States by
Cardinal Publishers Group
7301 Georgetown Road, Suite 118
Indianapolis, Indiana 46268
www.cardinalpub.com

For Scott — my partner in fishing, love, and life

Table of Contents

*Embraced by the expansive beauty and crystal-clear
waters of the Lower Laguna Madre*

Acknowledgments

Many people have assisted in one way or another with this project.

I relied heavily on the expertise of my husband and teacher, Scott. He's taken time out of his schedule, which also included his own book deadline, to review this manuscript and offer some very helpful edits. He encouraged me to put all else aside until this project was complete. Without him, I would not be fly fishing; I would not know about South Texas or the Lower Laguna Madre; and I would not be writing this book. His encouragement and support are like a fine gemstone — priceless. With Scott, I am living my dream.

My dear friend and angling mentor, Wanda Taylor, has been an invaluable cheerleader. Hailing from Tennessee, she and her husband Gary operate fly fishing schools for both fresh and saltwater. She's listened to my vision for this book and celebrated its evolution. She's also encouraged me to get out there and "strut my stuff." I have in ways beyond my wildest imagination. We met the Taylors in October 1999, and through our meeting them, doors have magically opened for others to come into our lives, including Jeffrey Pill, producer of the video *Coastal Fly Fishing with Ken Hanley and Friends*. Jeff has become a good friend and a wonderful supporter of our work at Kingfisher.

Captain Skipper Ray has been an incredible mentor and friend to Scott and me. He taught me to see trout — a big feat. At each level of my development as a fly fisher and a guide, he always speaks some words of wisdom at precisely the right moment.

Fred Arbona has a passion for the Lower Laguna — and for redfish — that is infectious. The man possesses wealth of knowledge, which he has graciously shared with us both on and off the water.

Sister angler Cyndi Arbona has delighted me with visits to Kingfisher while her husband Fred sets up his yearly vigil on the LLM. We have been known to take over the dock and cast until the bewitching hour, while the men occupy the bank (our porch). Cyndi's presence brings much-needed female energy to the Inn (I hang out with the guys a lot), and helps me to remember the dream I had when I first arrived in Arroyo City. In my dream the ladies in the neighborhood came out at night and took over the water, swimming unabashedly naked in the moonlight. I believe this dream was urging me to embrace my fly rod and my place on the water on a much deeper level. And while I've never fly fished naked, there have been moments where I felt as if I was — especially in those earlier days.

Constance Whiston and other members of the Texas Women Fly Fishers honored me with an invitation to speak in 2001. It was in front of these women, and the gentlemen anglers in attendance, that I took my place as an "elder," in the community. I allowed the knowledge I have about the fly fishing on the Lower Laguna Madre to come forth. This event took me to a new level in my development.

My new friend Captain Sally Moffett from Rockport, Texas, stepped forward on our very first meeting at the Shallow Water Expo in Houston in the spring of 2002 and encouraged me to banish my fears and get my captain's license. Within a head-spinning couple of weeks, everything magically fell into place and I entered Kelley's Maritime Training Center on South Padre Island. For two weeks, I was under the tutelage of Captain Pat Kelley, and with his astute teaching methods, he assisted me in pulling off one of the greatest challenges of my life.

Each one of the clients that I've fished with — or listened to around the dinner table — has helped in their own unique ways. They know who they are, and I thank them wholeheartedly.

My children — Shana, Pete, and Ryan — have played their roles in my life to perfection, offering me the right amount of love, encouragement, and challenges to further me along on my path. They, along with others including numerous friends, have come into my life with divine timing and allowed me to work through my karma and learn valuable life lessons.

John and Shirley Mullins, my parents, have done this as well with their love, support, and patience, as they've witnessed my journey. They are to be applauded. I know they worry, especially when I accept new challenges that take me far from the nest. They deserve many thanks also for answering the numerous questions about my early childhood memories — both on and off the water.

Darla Christiansen Engelmann, my spiritual mentor, cannot be thanked enough. She's been there "in good times and bad," and patiently, sometimes firmly, encouraged me to keep growing. And most importantly, she's reminded me to tap into the Divine, and always act with love and integrity — no matter what I'm doing or what situations I face.

Maria Zamora is my ever-faithful assistant. She is more than a housekeeper, she's become my friend. She deserves kudos for all the effort she puts forth keeping order amidst the chaos of our creative efforts and the comings and goings of our guests.

My editor Natalie Chambers, with her lack of fly fishing experience and fresh spirit, has made this a better book.

Holly Kondras, publisher of Wish Publishing, deserves a big applause for her patience with the unfoldment of this project. While we've worked together for nearly a decade, perhaps more, this is the first time I've been in her stable of writers. Usually I have the honor of editing for her. I know I tried her patience with my pleas for just a little more time.

Most of all she needs to be honored for having the vision and courage to found Wish Publishing, a women's sports publishing house. Thank you for providing the forum for our voices to be heard.

Once again I thank all of you.

Kathy Sparrow
August 2002

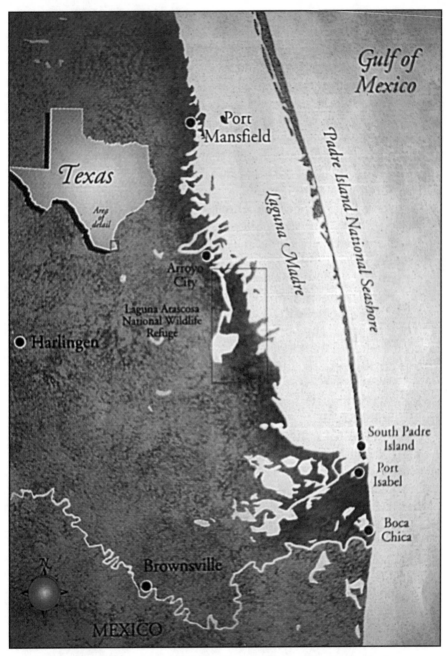

Map of South Texas, showing Lower Laguna Madre (Illustration by Larry Largay; reprint permission granted by Salt Water Fly Fishing*)*

The Initiation Begins

When I took up fly fishing I had no idea that it would become an integral part of my spiritual practice — my journey to self-development and self-mastery. I simply wanted to spend time with Scott on the water, gracefully perfecting my casting and catching techniques with a fly rod. My desire was to commune with nature and be relieved of some of the stress of life. I longed to be enveloped by the mantle of the expansiveness of the Lower Laguna Madre and enjoy a respite from my responsibilities for just a few hours a week.

While my forays into the Bay, as we affectionately call the Mother Lagoon, have provided me with just that, there were many challenging moments when much more was demanded of me than just showing up and casting my rod. Soon I realized each cast or each encounter with a fish or another inhabitant of the Lower Laguna Madre was a mirror of what was going on in my life — off the water. I needed the same discipline and commitment to become a serious fly fisher as I did on my journey to become one with God, or at least become a better person.

Joan Wulff, the legendary godmother of fly fishing, says, "[Fly] fishing is a test of your values."

Fly fishing has done this and more, as have other aspects of my spiritual practice. Yoga, for instance, demands the same concentration and presence as I need to cast my rod. It's vital to be aware of how my body is moving and what subtle change in form might be necessary to improve either asana (yoga postures) or cast. Meditation and prayer require one-pointed fo-

1

cus as well as the commitment and daily discipline to set aside time to do my practice. Casting demands the same. Ultimately I've found that these independent practices compliment one another and provide me with a cumulative benefit that affects all areas of my life.

Baron Baptiste, author of *Journey into Power*, said "Yoga is ultimately a journey into truth about who you really are, what you are capable of, how your actions affect your life....It brings up everything that's in there — the fears, doubts, frustrations, toxins, strengths, beliefs."

He might as well be talking about fly fishing, especially saltwater fly fishing. The Laguna Madre has provided me with numerous opportunities where I have been coaxed, sometimes pushed, out of my comfort zone. She's taught me what I am truly capable of whether I'm wielding my rod or manning my boat. This in turn has given me more confidence in my other roles as well.

Pandit Rajamani Tigunait, spiritual head of the Himalayan Institute, said, "Because human beings reflect an extraordinary range of physical, mental, and emotional capacities, there is no single yoga practice or set of practices that will serve to awaken the yoga shakti [divine consciousness] in everyone."

Fly fishing has awakened something inside of me that has allowed me to forge a closer connection to the Divine. It's a presence that's palpable whether I'm off alone wading the flats or patiently working with a novice on the finer points of casting a fly rod to a pod of tailing redfish. I can best describe it as a mantle of comfort infused with an energy that makes me feel very much alive and content.

British scholar and author of many books including *The Chronicles of Narnia*, C.S. Lewis said, "We are told that all must come to the Father through Jesus Christ, but we're not told how that's going to happen." Here he referred to the necessity of a variety of paths, all leading to the same Source.

I, too, believe God knows that we need all the help we can get to come home again — to remember who he truly wishes us to be, and to live our true authentic lives. That is why he has sent a great many teachers — Jesus, Buddha, the Holy

Mother, and so many others and most likely continues to do so.

He also gave us fly fishing, and he lured me to the Lower Laguna Madre.

In some ways I'm shocked. I often wonder how I wound up in South Texas owning a fly fishing lodge. On occasion, I've chuckled aloud and looked toward the sky and asked, "Who wrote this script?"

On the other hand, I'm really not surprised. Looking over the last two decades that have led to this time and place, I can distinguish a fine thread woven in the fabric of my life. My yearning to understand the greater meaning of life and where I fit within the grand scheme of things has been my focus for many decades, long before I picked up a fly rod. Relying on the foundation of my Roman Catholic background, I explored Native American spirituality, earth-based religions, and many Eastern traditions. In college I could not get enough of my Religion of the World class. I yearned to know more about God, to know more about myself, and to most of all improve myself so that in all situations I could be a channel for God's love. It's been a rough road at times.

I've been tried and tested beyond my wildest imagination. In moments of self-pity, I've often imagined tarring and feathering those who have tried to console me with Nietzsche's famous dictum, "If it doesn't kill you, it will make you stronger."

However, I've also experienced times of true bliss. These moments are worth all the effort I put into my traditional spiritual practice.

While my fly fishing apprenticeship has thus far spanned five years as of this writing, my commitment to this sport equals that of my spiritual practice. There is no turning back for me. I'd no sooner pick up a spinning rod (frequently referred to as conventional tackle) or chuck a piece of mullet (a bait fish used to catch game fish) than I would go back to polluting my mind, body, and spirit with that which I know is not good for me. I yearn for a purer, simpler way of being, one that urges me to become the best of who I am, and demands complete, unadulterated commitment.

3

Saltwater fly fishing demands all of that and more. No half-way measures are allowed. Around every corner, with every step, and with every cast, there lies yet another test, and you must meet the challenge head on if you want to feel accomplished. It's like life in its fullest.

My initiation into fly fishing began long before I met Scott or picked up a fly rod. My connection with nature has always been very strong. I grew up in a rural area of Upstate New York, in the Hudson Valley, where dairy farms and apple orchards abound — or they did during my childhood days. My playground consisted of a nearby stream and open fields where wheat and corn were grown by a local farmer.

I have many memories of taking long walks with my parents after an evening meal into those fields where my younger brother and I would race ahead as my little sister watched from her perch upon my father's shoulders. Jumping bogs in the swamps was a favorite activity. We would hop from one to another, and inevitably walk home with at least one wet shoe. During the winter, our jaunts into those fields usually went hand-in-hand with a hunting trip. My brother and I would sit quietly next to my father, usually on a fallen tree, and wait patiently for the squirrels to meet their maker. I was fascinated by the many different tracks left by the animals, and before I was too far along in years, I could easily identify the trails of mice, raccoons, rabbits, deer, and squirrels. After a time I felt I knew where their homes were, which standing tree or fallen log was their favorite. I could tell if they traveled alone or in the company of others. Little did I know that I was developing a skill I would need as a fly fisher. In addition to being able to read the telltale signs of a creature's presence, I was developing a greater awareness of my surroundings, which now enables me to detect the subtle clues of the presence of fish or stingrays.

Much of my childhood was also spent on the water. I accompanied my father and my neighbors — Uncle Ed and Dale — on ice-fishing trips on Copake Lake. I remember peering down into the water, noticing the thickness of the ice, and the telltale bend of the ice-fishing rig as perch tugged at the line. The high point, however, was sneaking off to the fire to get warm and drink the hot chocolate, made from Ovaltine. My brother and I could have all that we wanted.

On Saturday mornings in the warmer weather, I watched as my maternal grandfather patiently went through the trunk of his car, readying his gear for his treks into the nearby streams. Shortly after meeting Scott, my parents reminded me that he fly fished. We now have many of his original flies safely tucked away.

With my paternal grandfather, I ran trot lines on the East Fork of the White River in a little place called Shoals, Indiana. The land where my grandparents' two-room-sans-plumbing cabin rested is now part of the Hoosier National Forest. We caught catfish and white perch, along with gar and buffalo. My grandmother fried them to perfection for the evening meal. She canned the extra, which she took back to New York at the end of their summer stay in Indiana.

During the day, we seined areas of the river for bait — crawfish — with my second cousins. I remember a time when the other women in the family — my mother and great-aunts — joined us on a hunt for mussels, which were also used for bait. We jumped out of the boat in an area where the water ran about waist-deep to a 10-year old, and with our bare feet, we searched the pebbly bottom for mussels. When one was found, we crimped our toes around it and brought our find to the surface. On one memorable occasion, my mother found several freshwater pearls in one of the mussels.

In our own backyard, just a short hike through the community cemetery, we had a favorite swimming hole, which we called Biddy's. It provided a refreshing treat on hot summer days, when central air was unheard of, especially in the north. My siblings, friends, and I, along with my mother, would either ride our bikes or walk hastily to the water, usually with our inner tubes in tow. Sneakers protected our feet from broken glass. Biddy's was also the spot for teenagers to go drinking and parking.

Biddy's was located on a prime trout stream, North Creek (up north we pronounce this "crick"). When we weren't swimming, we fished. Actually I remember watching more than fishing. As my father and grandfather worked the stream, I could see the trout rising and began to spot their bodies beneath the water. From the bank of my childhood home waters, I watched and I learned, and tucked all that knowledge away for some future time.

Then some thirty plus years later, after many years of living in cities, with only an occasional foray into the woods on an afternoon hike, I returned to the water, not as an observer, but as an active participant.

In the early months of my new life, which symbolically commenced with the ending of my first marriage, I met Scott Sparrow and I began my initiation into a higher order of anglers. During the spring of 1997, when Scott and I first began dating, we spent many of our dates upon the water in Rudee Inlet in Virginia Beach, where we were living at the time. I usually brought along a book and my journal while Scott fished for our dinner. A month or so into our relationship, we were taking our children — his 8-year-old-son Ryan and my 19-year-old daughter Shana on a fishing excursion. My plan was to sit and watch, take pictures, and of course, read or journal. But God had other plans for me that day.

It was cloudy and cool when we set out, and rain was in the air. I could smell it. But our kids insisted that they wanted to go as planned. As we launched the boat, a light and pleasant sprinkle began. Ryan and Shana urged us onward. So we headed out and found a spot known for flounder. As Scott rigged up the kids' rods, I sat on the seat and watched. The sprinkles gave way to a steady rain so there was no point in bringing out a book that would only get wet. Shana and Ryan each hooked up quickly and excitement filled the air. I snapped pictures while they brought their catch on board. I delighted in their successes.

Then without warning, Scott handed me a rod and urged me to cast. Despite my self-consciousness, I cast the baited line as far as I could and slowly reeled the jig — a lure comprised of a lead head on a single hook and a plastic worm-like body. I repeated the action over and over. It wasn't long before I reached success and brought a flounder onto the boat. Scott took him off the hook and threw him into the ice chest. I winced hearing it flip flop around until the ice lulled it into an endless slumber. I had just contributed to supper.

The water in Rudee Inlet is cloudy. Never did we see our prey. Our catch consisted of flounder, trout, and an occasional puppy drum — also known as a redfish. We never knew what was on the end of our lines until we reeled it in. But it was a start. I'd gotten off the bank and I was now a fisher.

My Introduction to the Mother Lagoon

August 1997. I flew to the Rio Grande Valley in South Texas to be with Scott during the final ten days of his six-week retreat, which he had planned well before our paths had crossed. His mission was to write and meditate, and to find the big trout on the Lower Laguna Madre. My joining him represented an introduction not only his family and the land he calls home, but to his precious home waters as well. However, meeting the Laguna Madre held more than fishing experiences for me. It was through her that my relationship to the Divine Feminine was deeply forged.

Up until just a few years ago, my image of the Divine was strictly male. He appeared as a God that was very old, gentle, fatherly, and easily approachable. He even withstood my occasional tantrums when I raised my voice and shook my fist, stating very loudly and clearly that I'd had enough of whatever life was dishing out to me at the time. I felt his kind and gentle support through a variety of male models — whether it be Santa Claus during my childhood years, or through Jesus Christ with whom I developed an even closer relationship during the healing process of my divorce. God with all his divine splendor was the higher power in my life. The Divine Feminine was foreign to me.

I enjoyed notions of the fairy godmother and the tooth fairy, but these were part of my childhood fantasies and not to be taken seriously. Further, the Holy Mother was merely a statue on one side of the altar in my childhood church, whom was barely recognized as having any significant role in my spiri-

tual life, except at Christmas and a few other Catholic obser-
vances, referred to as "holy days of obligation." In addition,
my earlier education, and my employment in government,
emphasized the importance of supporting the male authority
figure. In high school I was channeled into a business tract,
learning support skills such as typing and shorthand that would
earn me meager employment opportunities as a secretary or
bookkeeper. My interest in writing and drama, both expres-
sions of my true Self were overlooked. In my midtwenties, I
worked as a staff assistant for a congressman in a system that
was very patriarchal, although my contributions as the youngest
female staff member running a district office were significantly
acknowledged. In my first marriage, my "place" was regarded
as secondary. My role was to perform my duties as a wife and
mother; my work and financial contributions to the family were
considered insignificant and often dismissed. While I have a
strong mother, in retrospect she often appeared stuck in her
role as caretaker of my grandfather, my father, my siblings,
and me. She frequently fled to the outside world to volunteer
at the hospital or to bowl as an expression of her freedom apart
from her role in the household.

No matter where I turned, the scales were unbalanced, and
definitely favoring the often unhealthy masculine forces in my
life. No where could I find evidence of the importance of honoring the Divine Mother. Nor was I awake enough in my youth
to seek her out. But slowly over the years, the Divine Feminine
appeared, attempting to provide me with a more balanced and
healthier view of life. I let down my guard a little at a time and
accepted her teachings. Through nature, she made me aware
that most young animals and birds are raised by both parents.
And it is the strong, loving mother, who tosses the young out
into the world, with support and faith in their ability to sur-
vive. While I've never doubted her love for me, my mom, whose
own mother was physically and emotionally absent in her life
due to mental illness, didn't have the skills to provide me with
the direction to leave the nest at the proper stage in my own
development. I fled in my late teens, lacking the wisdom and
maturity to enter adulthood gracefully, and made some very

poor choices. Subconsciously, however, I must have felt the Divine Mother's absence, for I've had older women enter my life and play the role of godmother, in the various cities that I've lived, far from my own mother. Robert Johnson, author of *Balancing Heaven and Earth: A Memoir* wrote, "We need godparents to finish our emotional and spiritual education. No two parents, however skilled or developed can do all of that for a young person."

Then I began having a direct relationship with the Divine Feminine.

The Divine Mother never forced herself upon me. Instead she made her presence known with patience and compassion. In my twenties, I participated in moon circles where my friends and I chanted and drummed, honoring the feminine aspects of the higher power. But I didn't feel completely comfortable with the process. I went through the motions, but nothing happened to make me feel deeply devoted to a feminine force. The overpowering masculine influence in my life weighed heavily upon me. I struggled with the dogma of my childhood religion and feared that my actions would be construed as having false gods before me. It was also difficult for me to do as my mother did — to find the freedom to express my individuality outside of my household duties. Surrendering to the feminine face of God was a constant battle, until Sunday, October 20, 1996, when the Blessed Mother Mary came into my life, paving the way for other manifestations of the Divine Feminine to enter.

During a post-separation trip to Indiana I severely injured my knee in fall from the top bunk in my daughter's dorm. The phone rang in the middle of the night, and I instinctively jumped out of bed to answer it, forgetting that I was five feet off the ground. When I landed there was a loud pop, and I fell to the ground knowing that my injury was not a simple sprain. The physical pain matched the emotional pain that I was feeling, for it was just hours before, that my son Pete made it absolutely clear that he wanted to remain with his father. I was to return to Virginia Beach, with only my belongings, leaving behind my two children — Shana in college, and Pete still in high school. I was at a crossroads and I faced starting a new life in a very different role — that of a single woman, with literally no one to care for but myself. In the morning light, as I made arrangements to vacate my storage unit and rent a small moving van, I was aware that my 10-hour drive back to my new home was only the beginning of my journey. The work of healing, both physically and emotionally, was about to begin. I had no idea what was in store for me. It was scary and exciting at the same time.

The pain in my knee was excruciating at times. I hobbled to work, keeping my knee propped up under my desk at the A.R.E. — the Association for Research and Enlightenment, an organization dedicated to preserving and enhancing the work begun by Edgar Cayce, best known for his psychic medical readings. I was an editor and writer in the publishing department of the organization and had access to a network of holistically minded medical providers. However, due to the severity of my injury even my holistic physician suggested surgery. I quickly dismissed his recommendation. I had only recently moved into my new second-floor apartment, knew no one that I could rely on for transportation to my new job, or who I could depend upon to walk my dog on a regular basis. I was on my own and feeling very much alone. I had to opt for less restrictive avenues of healing: massage, castor oil packs, and laying-on-of-hands — a spiritual healing technique where divine energy is channeled through the healer's hands. Slowly I began experiencing relief, and I was able to resume my long walks on the beach of the Chesapeake Bay each morning and evening — a ritual which helped me in the process of my emotional healing.

One evening I was walking along the beach, and I began experiencing a deep ache in the center of my injured knee. I wasn't surprised, as I had just spent the better part of an afternoon circle dancing with a group of spiritual seekers under the direction of Matthew Fox, a Dominican priest, and founding director of the Institute in Culture and Creation Spirituality. However, as I walked along the beach with my dog, mesmerized by the lapping of the small waves against the shoreline, the image of a hole in my heart appeared in my mind, and somehow I knew that the discomfort in my knee and my heart were connected. Later at the evening lecture, I made an appointment for the following afternoon for a laying-on-of-hands treatment.

At the beginning of the treatment I lay quietly on the massage table praying for healing. I immediately felt the presence of Jesus in the room, and tears welled up in my eyes. I said nothing to the woman healer whose hands hovered above my knee. Then I felt Jesus lay his hands upon my heart, and I was drawn into a deep meditative state. Within moments, I felt another presence holding my feet, and saw in my mind's eye the Holy Mother standing at the foot of the massage table. By this time, I was crying. I felt as if he was taking large pieces of pain from my chest. Jesus then leaned over and said to me, "Giveth to me all your pain and sorrow. You will be persecuted no more." I was completely enveloped in their love, and I felt so "at home." I wanted to stay there with them, but I had to go back to my body, which by this time was very cold. Slowly I returned, sobbing so deeply — not from the emotional pain regarding the issues with my children and my ex, but because I was separating from Jesus and Mary.

The healer was a bit concerned since she felt the drop in my body temperature. After wrapping me with a blanket, I told her briefly of my experience. It was difficult to tell. I just wanted to go home and be alone with it. I left there feeling very much "in love with God." But more so, I now knew the Divine Mother and completely trusted her presence in my life. Through her presence I realized the importance of the feminine aspects of the divine power, and I began seeing evidence of her influence in the world. This was particularly noticeable in nature, especially in my connection with the Laguna Madre.

The Lower Laguna Madre is an exquisite natural treasure. The vast estuary extends in all directions beyond the thin line where the sky and water meet. The horizon is only occasionally broken by small islands, which serve as rookeries, or nesting grounds, for birds in all shapes and sizes. The water itself is gin-clear and shallow, about knee deep or less in most places,

Only a thin line between sky and water is visible on calm mornings on the Lower Laguna Madre.

with the deepest areas running no more than three feet. Being here truly brings you closer to God and to your own true Self. Little did I know in the sweltering August heat that the Bay would become an undeniable force in my life.

The Lower Laguna is a virtually landlocked hypersaline lagoon that is bordered on the east by Padre Island (the longest barrier island in the world), and on the west by the King Ranch and Laguna Atascosa National Wildlife Refuge, two vast expanses of land holdings that prevent development along the Bay's shorelines. It has two manmade openings to the Gulf of Mexico, one near Port Mansfield to the north, and the other near Port Isabel to the south. A manmade channel, referred to as the Land Cut, at its northern end joins the Lower Laguna to the Upper Laguna. The largest continuous shallow water flat in North America, the Lower Laguna Madre is largely unaffected by modern encroachment, and has a primitive beauty that is rare in today's world. It is approximately 350 square miles in size, and about three-fourths of it is too shallow for most fishing boats. Until recently, it was virtually unknown to fly fishers. Today, it is referred to as the least pressured and most available saltwater fly fishery in the country.

The LLM is the only true subtropical fishery in the continental United States, except for south Florida. There are a variety of fishing venues, which include grass-bottom lagoons and flats, and a vegetation-free flat called the "white sand," which resembles the Bahamas in its clarity and vastness. It is the only place in the world where you can frequently sight cast to world record spotted sea trout. Four of the current International Game Fish Association (IGFA) world records were caught on the LLM, with others pending. The species of catchable fish include the red drum (redfish), spotted sea trout (speckled trout), black drum, sheepshead, tarpon, ladyfish (skipjack), jack crevalle, and flounder.

When you enter a relationship with the Lower Laguna with a fly rod, your life subtly changes. As a teacher, she really expects nothing but the best from you. She is mentor, friend, and devil's advocate all wrapped up into one. She has made her way into my heart and into my life so deeply that she has replaced the childhood swimming hole I once knew as my home waters. Indeed, I feel that I have finally found my true home. The Lower Laguna Madre has taught me to let go of predictability and routine. Change is a constant in life, and the Mother Lagoon reminds us of this every single day. If she fishes well in one section one day, there's no guarantee you'll even see a single fish in that same location the next.

Her nature fluctuates with the tides and the winds. With her rich aromas varying from sweet salty air to the deep stench of decay, she never lets me forget that success and failure, life and death, go hand in hand. There are places where walking in her is like walking in an aquarium — with a firm, sandy bottom and an occasional patch of grass to provide shelter for minnows, crabs, and shrimp. Here you can see the wonderful coppery redfish swimming along from yards away in shin-deep water. Wading on this particular bottom is like a walk in the park. Then there are areas in the Mother Lagoon where you can sink to your thighs in the soft, silty bottom in a blink of an eye. With each step you wonder if it will be your last — or if you'll have the strength to make your way back to the boat. Stealthy wading is nearly impossible because of the noise you make prying yourself from her grasp. Kayaks are often in order for these venues.

The Lower Laguna Madre operates under the highest laws—those of nature, those of God—and she doesn't let me get away with anything less than I am truly capable of giving and doing. But during my first days on the water, I had no idea that these were things I'd realize only in hindsight.

During that August trip, I watched Scott gracefully and artfully catch beautiful big fish on his rod. I discovered two truths: One, I needed to learn to fly fish, and Two — with or without him, I was going to make my home on this beautiful estuary. Within days of returning to Virginia, I asked Scott to give me lessons, and I began practicing on the front lawn. Within six months, we were married, and our plan unfolded to make yet another leap of faith — to live on the Lower Laguna. In August of 1999, just two years after I first set eyes on the Bay, we moved into our home, and shortly thereafter opened Kingfisher Inn in Arroyo City. Within three years of being in business, I've gone from being a hostess and recreational fly fisher to a fully-licensed guide, having passed the much dreaded Coast Guard exam and screening process that conveys the privilege of taking out other fly fishers for hire.

The Mother Lagoon has not let me rest on my laurels. Each time I go out onto the Bay, I anticipate some teaching, and that in itself is as exciting as catching fish. Sometimes the teacher appears as a redfish, a trout, a stingray, an egret, or even as a soft whispering voice, which leads me lovingly, although not always gently, into some greater understanding of myself and of the whole of life.

As with all spiritual practices, fly fishing has provided me not only with beautiful vistas, but also dark, lonely nights. While meaningful, my development as a saltwater fly fisher has been as painful as it has been joyous. When I think back to all my frustrations and utter failures and embarrassments, it's a wonder I didn't put my rod down and go back to sitting on the bank. But somehow I kept going. Something within me drove me onward, and it can probably be likened to that same inner yearning that keeps me true to the traditional spiritual disciplines that I embrace — yoga, meditation, praying the rosary, and eating a healthy diet. Ultimately, what I desire is to be free of all the issues that dampen my days with anger, fear, thoughts of revenge, and other afflictions of a fragile ego. But those of us who have actively chosen to partake in some form of self-evaluation know that it's an arduous journey, at times filled with wonderful rewards. Over time, it gets easier. Learning to fly fish on the Laguna Madre has proven to be no exception.

Fly fishing expert Lani Waller caught his first redfish on a fly rod during the filming of the Texas segment of *Coastal Fly Fishing with Ken Hanley and Friends*. "This is among the most technically demanding fly fishing I've ever encountered." Lani was baffled, even after having fly fished all around the world. "It's the complexity that makes it so interesting, so exciting, and so rewarding when you do succeed."

His comment was music to my ears. I thought I was the only person who ever took six months of regular fishing to catch her first redfish. I had seriously considered that I just didn't have what it took to be a saltwater fly angler.

In truth it was the Divine Mother gently coaxing me to unfurl the potentials that had lain dormant within me, and to become a more complete person.

Befriending My Fears

August 1997. On my first trip to the Laguna Madre, as I eased over the side of the boat, I became immediately aware of the warmth of the water. It was a significant contrast to the frigid temperature of my childhood home waters.

I'd never waded in an aquarium before, and this was a very large one. It was teeming with life — lots of it. And like life in its fullness, there came with it the good and the bad. The "good" were the gamefish that Scott and I were aiming to find and catch. The "bad," a force that I had to reckon with, were the stingrays. According to Joseph C. Britton and Brian Morton, authors of *Shore Ecology of the Gulf of Mexico*, "At least six species of stingrays are known to occur in Texas waters, but two are common. The Atlantic stingray... and the southern stingray."

Both are bottom feeders. They follow anglers, and accompany redfish and trout in their foraging for food. When they're not on the prowl, they bury themselves in the muddy or sandy bottom of the Bay. Herein lies the danger. You often cannot see them, making it easy to accidentally step upon them. The dark-brown cownose ray is less of a threat, even though it is armed with the same stinging barb as its cousins. We see them frequently during the summer months, swimming in schools across the east side of the Bay. Resembling a small manta ray, they are graceful, beautiful, and are known to jump out of the water, although I've yet to witness this.

I'd heard the stories of stingrays well before my arrival. I'd been warned to shuffle my feet repeatedly, to avoid stepping

My friend the Stingray—"God's First Angel"

on one. The barb on their tail is filled with a marine poison, and the sting is said to be so painful it's likened to being stabbed with a hot knife. Before entering the water, I heard a tale or two of men and women being laid up for months with this injury, and the ensuing infections that often go hand-in-hand with being stung. These stories didn't give me much peace of mind as I took my first step out of the boat.

My first shuffle in the water filled my wading shoes with a pound of silt. Before long, I felt like I was wearing concrete booties. Prior to his guiding days, Scott ventured into any water, with a hard or soft bottom, as long as there were fish. He was the master fisherman, and so I followed. I shuffled and shuffled until I was far enough away from the boat to begin casting my line. Not knowing exactly what I was looking for in the water, I began blind casting, focusing on every ripple, hoping to spot a tailing red. Scott's son Ryan had told me to look for the large black dot on their tails. His information later proved to be helpful.

I became engrossed in my activity, forgetting I was in the middle of one of the largest saltwater estuaries in the world. Then I caught a glimpse of pinkish flesh out of the corner of my eye. It wasn't a redfish. I froze. My heart raced and I desperately longed to be back on the boat. I turned around to see if I could easily wander back without drawing too much attention to myself. Somehow I had waded so far from the boat that it was barely visible. Scott was ahead of me, engrossed in his own fishing. Worse yet, we were accompanied by his brother and nephew. Being newly introduced to the family, I didn't want to give them the impression that I was a wimpy girl tagging along. I refrained from screaming. I poked the stingray with my rod and it scurried away. I returned to fishing, still shaken by my close encounter.

That night I had a dream — the first of many about stingrays. I was on a boat with Scott. There were stingrays around the boat and I became fearful. I wasn't about to get out and go fishing. Then a voice boomed through my dream consciousness — I knew to listen and listen closely. The voice said, "The stingrays are God's first angels." I entered the water the next day pondering that dream, yet ever aware that I may encounter one of these "angels" with any false step that I made. I repeated my mantra—*I will never let fear prevent me from fully living ever again!* It was a promise I'd made to myself after leaving my first marriage—frequently referred to as my past life. It was an era when my fears prevented me from taking steps toward leading a healthier, happier life. Another dream followed shortly after we returned to Virginia Beach. I was once again on a boat, this time alone, and there were stingrays around the boat. Several were reaching out to me, and they were begging to be fed. I reached out to touch them in the dream, but woke before making contact.

Besides being a master fly fisher, Scott is also a master at dream interpretation. His dissertation at William and Mary explored the phenomenon of lucid dreaming, or the experience of becoming fully aware that one is dreaming during the dream. Later, given the amazing creative capabilities that lucidity confers, he became convinced that the symbolism in our dreams is not as important as our responses in the dream, regardless of whether we're actually aware that we're dreaming or not. Based on this criterion of success, my sequence of dreams indicated that I was making progress. At first my fearfulness prompted a stern but loving response from the Divine that stingrays are a part of God's creations, just as I am. In the last dream, despite my fear, I reach out to touch the stingray. Even though the dream ended before I could make contact, I had crossed the threshold of realizing what Rilke once said: "Perhaps everything which is terrible is, in the final analysis, only something that wants our love."

That first step is one I'll never forget, no matter how much time has passed. I faced my fear and got "off the bank." In doing so, I embraced the Laguna Madre as my mentor and teacher. I did not know exactly what I had agreed to, nor if I consciously agreed to anything at all. But she's taught me more about life and about myself than I could have ever hoped for. Each time I enter the Bay, I learn a little bit more. She holds up a mirror for me to look within and recognize those traits that prevent me from being all that I'm meant to be.

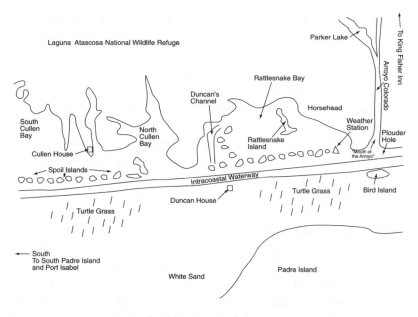

South of the Mouth of the Arroyo

There is a Cheyenne saying, "What occurs around you and within you reflects your own mind and shows you the dream you are weaving."

In those initial days, the Mother Lagoon was merely mirroring my proclivity to fear through the encounters with the stingrays. It was a major challenge to overcome the psychological pattern of allowing fear to dominate my life and thereby negatively influence the choices I made. In the early days of my new life, following the demise of my first marriage, the Divine Mother had to provide me with circumstances whereby I could learn to make different choices, ones that allowed me to move past my fear. It was up to me to respond appropriately and in a more balanced psychologically and spiritually healthy manner. I could choose to weave a fearless lifestyle, or continue to be trapped in the nightmare of unnecessary and often unhealthy limitations created by the fearful side of myself. It was a deep-seated pattern that I knew would take innumerable circumstances for healthy responses to become second-nature.

Dr. Jean Shinoda Bolen, best known for her book *Goddesses in Every Woman*, said, "Life presents us with repeated opportunities to face what we fear, what we need to become conscious of, or what we need to master."

I've had repeated opportunities. One day Scott and I were wading from Rattlesnake Island to the shoreline of Horsehead. I was not thinking of fishing, but obsessing over the difficulties of my post-divorce issues. I was invested body, mind, and soul when a flutter and a whap against my wading boot caused me to wake up and take notice. I gasped and my heart raced feverishly. I came terribly close to stepping on a stingray. I looked down and a mud trail was the only evidence of the winged creature's hit and run. God was sending me a message via his angel to come back to the present. My make-believe world, with its unmanifested threats, was overshadowing my real world. I wasn't fishing. I was taking up space, going through the motions (pitifully I might add). So needless to say I didn't catch fish. Nor did I for the remainder of the day. I allowed my mind to poison my present experience, which had a ripple affect throughout the rest of my day — no matter how I tried to reign my mind back into alignment with the water, the fish, and my body. I'm ashamed to admit that it's something I did often in meditation as well, thereby mitigating any benefit of sitting still with my eyes closed for an hour or so.

My challenge was not to will my ex off the face of the planet. I had tried that many, many times, and it didn't work. The real test was to change my response to any apparent attempt he made to disrupt the peace and harmony of my present life. That was the hurdle I had to clear with anyone I saw as the "enemy" — be it insurance companies, lawyers, the ex's — or stingrays. And it took my encounters with a creature who could do real harm to me — if I made the wrong step — to learn this lesson. This was the main obstacle I had to face if I was to master saltwater fly fishing. I had to change my response to the stingray if I was going to be comfortable enough to be aware of its presence and yet remain focused on the task at hand — catching a fish with my fly rod. If I couldn't reach that level of comfort, I might as well stay on the bank, frozen in fear. I knew this wasn't an option.

When living in Connecticut I met a Hedda Leonard, a healer, while doing a magazine assignment. I was so taken with her presence that I became one of her clients. As she poked and prodded my body back into alignment we became friends. Her loving support helped me stay afloat during some difficult moments. She shared with me some profound wisdom that I remember whenever I'm faced with difficult situations: "Stay in the moment, meet people where they are, and act accordingly."

I also needed good information. Good counsel allay many of my fears about the legal matters. I also had misconceptions about the stingray that needed to be corrected. I feared that I could be zapped by their barb just by passing by them. It took almost four years to learn the truth about my winged friends.

Scott and I were out one winter day fishing with our friend Skipper Ray. (No he does not sport wings, and his laconical manner makes him far from an angel, but we love him anyway.) We were blind casting in Parker Lake, an expanse of water on the south side the Arroyo Colorado, not far from the mouth. A flounder fluttering by segued our conversation into stingrays. There I learned that you did not get stung by a stingray unless you stepped directly on them. By this time I knew that they didn't attack, but I still believed that I could get sideswiped by one and end up in a deeply painful situation. Scott may be a great teacher, but he left out this precious bit of information that quite possibly could have saved me years of fretting. I've learned to ask questions, especially if it can shorten my learning curve.

For guests and friends about to embark for a day of fishing on the Bay, I recite the morning mantra: "Shuffle your feet, don't step backwards, and don't walk back to the boat in your mud trail." I repeat it often to myself as well.

Skipper told me that most people get stung while fighting fish. You need to adopt a global awareness of your surroundings while having one-pointed focus to fight your fish. Stingrays form symbiotic relations with wade fishers (and fish), and will follow in your mud trail, hoping you will stir something out of the bottom for them. There are many products on the market which provide additional protection, such as Kevlar-reinforced booties and stingray guards. Unfortunately, comfort is often sacrificed for protection. These products tend to be bulkier, heavier, and could hamper stealthy movement in the water. But they could also save you a lot of pain and suffering. The choice is yours.

For years Scott and I opted for comfort, relying on faith and careful observance of our surroundings. Then one morning in the predawn hours before a tournament Scott stepped on a stingray. He stayed in the water for 10 hours (not the wisest move, to which he readily admits) so as not to ruin the day for our friend who had driven five hours from San Antonio to fish with Scott. The wound became infected with a dangerous marine bacteria — Vibrio vulnificus, prevalently found in stagnant tropical waters. Twenty-five percent of the people who become infected with this bacteria via a wound succumb to the infection or lose a limb. Vibriosis is most often contracted by eating seafood and usually results in gastroenteritis, in other words a bad stomach ache. Scott's infection was much more serious. After a very scary 10 days, we vowed to wear whatever protection was available so as not to be put through that test again.

However, if the unthinkable does happen, there are steps to take before you can get off the water and into town. Hot water expelled by the boat motor's water pump is an immediate source of relief for the pain. Meat tenderizer applied in paste-form is also helpful, as is taking a hefty dose of ibuprofen. Some say 1600 milligrams, but check with your health professional to be sure. Aspirin is not a good choice because the toxin in the barb is an anticoagulant, and aspirin only increases the effect.

Captain Dan Coley, a fellow Arroyo City resident and one of the most experienced guides on the Lower Laguna Madre, recently shared a Cajun remedy known to neutralize the poison on the stingray's barb: Take one pound of coffee and boil it with one large onion cut into pieces. Soak the foot for 45 minutes morning and night for at least a week. To ward off the bacteria, he and veteran Bay fishermen use bleach to clean out the wounds from hooks, fins, and toothy critters.

Learning to change my response to the stingray was challenging. It took quite a while to tame my flight or fight response when one came in close proximity to me while I was fishing. I used the method that was most available and extremely simple to calm myself — the breath. By breathing deeply, slowing my heart rate, I soon became unaffected by their close proximity to me.

According to Swami Rama, author of *Science of Breath*, "...the relationship between the breath and mind is reciprocal." He and co-authors Rudolph Ballentine, M.D. and Alan Hymes, M.D., claim that "by changing the pattern of breathing we can transform the personality, for when the mind is disturbed, the breath is disturbed and becomes shallow, rapid, and uneven. By consciously making the breath deep, even, and regular, we will experience a noticeable release of tension, and an increased sense of relaxation and tranquility."

The breath is an incredible tool we can use whenever life presents us with challenges, for we know difficulties will always be with us.

In *Being Zen*, Ezra Bayda explains a story about a farmer who goes to Buddha complaining about his problems. Bayda wrote, "The Buddha answered, 'My teaching can't help with the 83 problems, but perhaps it can help with the 84th.... The 84th problem is that we don't want to have any problems."

I really expected my life along the Arroyo to be blissful, that I'd paid my dues, and left my problems behind. I was wrong. I know that other spiritual seekers often feel the same.

Bayda explains, "Although we may not know it, we all have the deep-seated belief that if we pursue a spiritual practice long and hard enough, our problems will disappear. Beneath this belief lies an even deeper one: Life should be free from pain."

Mine wasn't. The stress mounted daily, and new challenges were presented to me...like facing the stingray. In my sessions with my spiritual mentor Darla Christiansen Engelmann, she frequently reminded me that life is not fair. I railed against such proclamation. During the healing session I'd had for my injured knee, Jesus said to me, "Giveth unto me all your pain

25

and sorrow. You will be persecuted no more." I had his word, so why did the troubles continue? It took me four years to realize that his message to me was not a guarantee against further life difficulties, but a reminder that he would be with me through all of my difficulties. Stingrays, ex's, government agencies, willful children, and feisty puppies are all a part of my life. I had to accept that, learn to see them differently, and know that I'm not really alone in all of this that is the finely woven fabric of my life.

Over time, I began to feel camaraderie, and later compassion for these angels of the Bay. As in my dream, I soon began to feel the need to go so far as to reach out to them. Scott and I were out fishing in the Spring of 2001. We were on a mission for big trout. In addition to wanting to fish, he needed photos for an upcoming article. He soon caught a 24-inch trout. While he readied his cameras, I told it not to worry — that we intended to release it. I was in awe at its beauty and felt deeply connected to it. In essence I felt love for this fish. Out of the corner of my eye, I saw a stingray approach. He nestled into the bottom about two feet from us. Moments passed as he eyed the trout and me. I was taken aback by his curiosity. Instead of reaching out, I scolded him for being too close. He soon departed.

While it's taken a great deal of effort, I have come to see the helplessness in that which I fear — especially the stingray. They go their whole lives being feared. Many end up tail-less after taking a baited hook, and finding themselves at the end of a fisherman's line. The lucky ones live to tell of it, sans tail. To this day I regret my reaction to that curious stingray. For me, the right action would have been to reach down and touch its alien-like head. At the very least, I could have taken the love that I felt for the trout and sent in the form of a prayer in the direction of the stingray. I missed an opportunity that I can only hope will present itself again.

Jack Kornfield in *A Path with Heart* said, "Very often what nourishes our spirit is what brings us face to face with our greatest limitations and difficulties. To work with them requires courage of spirit and heart."

While I have yet to complete my work with the stingray, I have made progress. It has taken courage of both spirit and heart. I'm amazed when I witness my growth through my reactions to those winged creatures. I'm saddened by the sight of their decaying bodies along the spoil banks. And I'm filled with compassion for those missing tails. Someday I hope to have the courage, not only to reach out, but to touch one.

Entering the Covenant

October 1997. Scott continued to work on his book about fly fishing, the quest for big trout, and the midlife passage, but in the process of writing about his family's past, he realized that his brother and he had offsetting strengths and fears. Scott had always been anxious about flying, while Chip had been an Air Force pilot and owned a high-performance plane capable of aerobatics. Similarly, Scott had wielded a fly rod since he'd been 12, but he'd been unable to convince Chip to take up the sport. In an attempt to forge a middle ground upon which they could become closer, Scott suggested a deal. He agreed to travel to Texas to do barrel rolls with Chip in his plane, if Chip agreed to fly fish with Scott. Chip caught the vision, and gladly agreed. So we headed south again for the second time that year.

Our first morning proved to be less than conducive for either fly fishing or flying, since an early cold front was blowing through the area. We opted to tour Laguna Atascosa National Wildlife Refuge located just ten miles or so from Rio Hondo. This preserve has over 45,000 acres and is growing in size as the government works with private foundations like The Nature Conservancy to ensure that some of the virgin South Texas brushland survives the encroachment of farming and development.

The primitive South Texas landscape is comprised of a variety of native tropical and desert trees and shrubs, such as mesquite trees, the thorny and golden-blossomed huisache trees, prickly pear cactus, Spanish Dagger and the rock-hard ebony trees. This austere and forbidding landscape provides home to the Texas Tortoise, green jays, javelina, road runners, and so much more. Out of the remaining 80 to 100 ocelots — a wild cat that is smaller than a bobcat — in the United States, 35 make their home at the Refuge. There are approximately 500 bird species that inhabit the area, either year-round or during migration periods, including the sandhill crane, the Aplomado falcon, and piping plovers.

From the very first visit in August of that year, Laguna Atascosa proved to be a mystical place for us, one that Scott discovered during his retreat. He was amazed that having lived in the Rio Grande Valley all of his childhood and early adult life that he'd never visited it. We had many magical wildlife encounters during our August stay. We watched an Aplomado falcon stoop over her prey and javelina — hairy, black pig-like creatures that emit a musky aroma detected from quite a distance — feast on prickly pear cactus. There was something about the land and its creatures that made my heart sing.

As we drove around the 15-mile Bay Drive, just one of the many trails at Atascosa, I sat in the back seat, Chip rode shotgun, and Scott was at the wheel. It was a blustery autumn day, and I was grateful for my fleece and windbreaker. The gray sky and the wind made it feel colder than it actually was. I only half-listened to the conversation floating toward me from the front seat. Instead, I focused my attention on the landscape — the coastal prairies, the grasslands, and the thorn forests.

We rounded a bend and I gazed out over a field of low brush. Something shifted inside me and I suddenly felt as if I was looking through someone else's eyes. I was actually seeing the landscape of the Refuge through another being's consciousness, and yet I was completely aware that it was happening. It was frightening at first, but also comforting. I couldn't move, I couldn't speak, I could only watch as we slowly made our way down the road.

I had the sense of experiencing the land in the distant past. Native American heritage is important to me. I studied some traditions early on in my spiritual seeking, and I have a great-great grandmother who was Cherokee. But never had I felt

South Texas landscape

"me," being overshadowed by some other soul force.

"Are you, okay?" Scott asked from the front seat.

I turned, and looked at him, still in a daze, but seeing him through my own eyes. "Yeah, fine." Those were the only words I could manage, as I felt drawn back into the altered state.

Later he said, "When I looked back at you, your face had changed. You looked very much like an Indian."

"I think I was." I went onto explain the shift in consciousness that I experienced.

I believe that this incident was confirmation of my connection to this area. All my life I had been searching for home, somewhere I felt truly comfortable. I spent thirty or so years in the Hudson Valley, a brief foray in Connecticut, and then four years in Indianapolis before moving to Virginia Beach. While I made myself comfortable, had friends and good work in each location, I was always yearning for something more — someplace to really settle in and be more of who I am. The night before Scott and I headed back to Virginia Beach during my first trip to South Texas, I stood on the dock saying good-bye to the land, the water, and its creatures. Tears welled up in my eyes unexpectedly. It was in that moment that I became aware that I had found my home. Seeing through the eyes of some other consciousness only cemented that feeling deeper into my soul.

I got my chance to fish the Bay wielding a fly rod within a day or so of that ride around Atascosa. As I entered the water, I was subtly aware that my movements changed. I no longer walked as though I was on pavement or around the house. Every step became deliberate, my senses heightened. I saw my surroundings more clearly and more attentively. I smelled everything around me — the salty air, the fishy silt bottom — and I heard the flutter of wings and the cries of the birds more sharply than in the past. I became a huntress, much like my Native American ancestors must have been.

Scott wandered off in search of his own fish, not wanting to get in either Chip's or my way. I had been practicing and while my cast was less than perfect, it was my intent that mattered most at this time. I gave it my best shot.

Spoil Islands

At one point I came upon a grassy edge near a spoil bank. The spoil islands, or spoil banks, are deposits of dredgings from the creation of the Intracoastal Waterway, which the Army Corp of Engineers dredged in the 1930s. The ICW is used not only for recreational boat traffic, but commercial fishermen and tugboats with barges, carrying cargo such as gasoline, grain, and benzene, traverse this waterway, which once was maintained from Maine to Texas. The spoil islands provide nesting sites for a variety of birds, and feeding areas for the gamefish. I saw redfish working the bank, moving along in search of food. Their backs were out of the water and their tails waved like ships' flags. They were unconcerned with my presence.

Chip was nearby and I felt myself hold back. I didn't want to get in his way. I encouraged him to join me and take his shot at the bounty before us. While he did venture toward me, he insisted that I take a shot. His gesture allowed me to feel like a peer. I felt embraced by the camaraderie of another fisher, someone other than Scott. I took my cast, actually several, but the fish just wouldn't pay attention to my presentation. It was less than perfect, but it was an attempt. Neither Chip nor I scored with our fly rod, but we did give it the old college try.

Map of Laguna Atascosa

We joined Scott at the boat (actually Chip's boat), compared notes, and made a plan for the next venue. At one point Chip pointed to a rod holder, and said, "I brought along a spinning rod for you in case you wanted back-up."

I shook my head. "No thanks. I'm here to fly fish."

Scott beamed at my dedication.

Henry David Thoreau said, "I know of no more encouraging fact that the unquestionable ability of man to elevate his life by conscious endeavor."

I made a conscious decision to learn this sport, and I was bound and determined to stick by it.

Redfish and speckled (or spotted) sea trout are the gamefish of choice for anglers on the Lower Laguna Madre. The most popular quarry for fly fishers is the red drum, or redfish. After the state of Texas designated redfish as gamefish, declaring them immune from commercial harvest once and for all, the population of redfish exploded in the Lower Laguna. Aided by the release of hatchery fingerlings into the Bay, the redfish numbers are as high as ever, and holding, providing fly fishers with ample opportunity to stalk fish from 3 to 10 pounds in clear, shallow conditions. Stalking is very much like hunting. We first see our prey and then go after them, casting to them only when they are within our reach.

Redfish live in the Bay from hatching until they reach spawning size, around 28 inches. It is then that they congregate near the passes to the open Gulf and lay their eggs in the late fall. As a rule, the spawning-size reds remain in the Gulf, but we sometimes catch fish in the 30- to 35-inch range in the Bay, as well.

Many fly fishers who have fished for bonefish say that redfish are definitely more challenging to catch. This might be surprising, given the redfish's reputation as a "blue-collar" bonefish. Bonefish traverse the flats in Florida and exotic tropical locations, and most fly fishers will travel for days to fish for this species. Redfish, up until late, have been seen as just a meager substitute for the bonefish. Fred Arbona—who has fished the world over—says that compared to redfish, bonefish are "boring and predictable," except perhaps in the Florida Keys where they've been pounded by flies.

While there can be days when redfish attack anything you throw at them, however poorly, they are as a rule very sensitive and quick to reject your presentation (your fly's placement on the surface of the water). Indeed, on the Lower Laguna, they are known to be unselective when it comes to fly pattern, but highly sensitive to poor presentations. So the rule of thumb is, if the fish rejects your fly, the presentation is at fault, not the fly.

Despite knowing how tough it was to lure a redfish to a fly, I never went back to the spinning rod — no matter how frustrating my attempts to hook-up on a fish became. After moving to our home on the banks of the Arroyo Colorado, Scott's father would call and ask for a report after each of our fishing excursions.

"Did you get your redfish yet?" he'd ask in his charming Alabamian drawl.

"No." I answered.

"Well maybe you ought to consider picking up that spinning rod again."

The thought horrified me, and I had to remind myself that his was not a malicious comment, nor was he questioning my ability. He merely wanted me to catch fish and in a way that was familiar to him. In all his 83+ years, he has not fly fished, and he's likely not to pick up the sport, although he thoroughly enjoys going out on the Bay with Scott or sitting on our dock catching small trout in the Arroyo.

When guests come to Kingfisher with the intention of fly fishing on the Bay, many for the very first time, Scott usually finds a way to let them know of my commitment to the sport and tells of my putting my spinning rod down and never turning back. Many squirm in their seats. But there are those whose eyes twinkle at the suggestion, intrigued by the challenge.

Other than cleaning around the spin rods that we have on hand for our fathers and our children, I haven't touched one since that August trip, several years back. I set my intention on learning to fly fish and I've stuck with it. Many of our guests have a spinning rod along, just in case. Just in case the wind is too high, just in case the fish are too spooky, just in case they get tired of casting. They hedge. I've discovered that there is no room for hedging in this sport — or in life in general — if you wish to have deep meaningful experiences. With fly fishing, you have to go into it all the way especially if you expect to achieve any degree of proficiency.

It's much the same on a spiritual path. You either surrender fully to the process, or you go through the motions and achieve no real breakthroughs on the path to enlightenment. Once you completely surrender, there is no going back on your path to oneness with God. Once the hook is set, there's no getting off the line.

In some of our many conversations about spirituality, my friend Berna remarked that there were many times when she wanted to jump off the spiritual path, concluding that ignorance is indeed bliss. But both maturity and experience have convinced both of us that once the covenant is made, there is no way to break the contract. You can never step foot off the path, even for a moment without dire consequences. A spiritual quest is not for "sissies," nor is fly fishing as my friend and fly fishing mentor Wanda Taylor says.

The urge to back out of a commitment occurs at difficult moments. This typically indicates a crossroads when if the right choice is made progress on the path is ensured. Both an overtly spiritual path and the fly fishing journey are filled with tests of commitment, courage, and perseverance.

In Eastern traditions, when one studies with a guru, the guru at some point usually puts the disciple through some test of their commitment before they consent to imbibe greater teachings upon the student.

For instance, when the great Tibetan guru Milarepa went to study with his teacher, Marpa, he faced a series of tests that would have turned most followers away. Marpa knew that Milarepa was full of pride, and a lust for power, and had to be humbled. Marpa began by having Milarepa construct a building, and then would tell him that he had built in the wrong place, or had done it all wrong. He would tell his disciple to tear it down and build it again. Whenever Milarepa asked Marpa for a formal initiation into his order, Marpa would scream at him, and throw him out of the temple. Unaware that Marpa would retreat to his quarters and weep over the pain that he had to inflict on his disciple, Milarepa even considered committing suicide at the depths of his ordeal. But he persisted in the face of humiliation and rejection, and eventually went on to become Marpa's successor.

The Mother Lagoon exhibits a similar capriciousness at times, and has put me through many tests — not only to my commitment to my spiritual path, but to fly fishing as well. Each time I was tempted to retreat into complacency, a little voice urged me to pick myself up by the boot straps and carry on. It truly is the only way I've gotten to where I am today, both on and off the water.

The Grace of the Fish God

September 1999. It was a day that started pretty much like any other — that is one that is planned for fishing. Scott rose first, started the coffee and began making the short trek to the dock with our gear. I rose, fighting the urge to sleep just awhile longer, knowing that his brother would soon be knocking on our door. I love fishing, but I also love sleeping. The two are often in conflict, and if it weren't for Scott gently urging me onward, I'd probably miss most early morning fishing experiences.

I stumbled through the house, sipping coffee, and dressing for the occasion, faithfully applying my sunscreen. We departed our dock just before the break of dawn and headed east from our place on the Arroyo Colorado toward the Lower Laguna Madre. I was typically silent saying a few prayers along the way for a safe journey along the waters and protection for our children, and an added one to protect me from my friends, the stingrays.

Our destination was Rattlesnake Bay, a shallow area, south of the mouth of the Arroyo, between a spoil bank along the ICW and the mainland shores of Laguna Atascosa National Wildlife Refuge. In the center of Rattlesnake Bay lies Rattlesnake Island. For years, Scott and Chip had spent a great deal of time stalking fish in this remote lagoon. We dropped Chip off near the mainland shoreline, referred to as Horsehead, that becomes the north bank of the lagoon. Scott and I putted the boat toward the middle of the lagoon so we could have a closer walk to Rattlesnake Island. I felt a sense of excitement rising in my veins that I hadn't felt before. *Perhaps today would be my lucky day — the day I'd catch my first redfish on a fly rod.* Scott had a plan to take me where he had scored big just several days before.

No matter how limited my success in terms of catching had been, I loved the sport. There is nothing more beautiful than being out on the Lower Laguna with the sun rising slowly in the sky, illuminating the spoil banks, cactus, and mangroves as it ascends the horizon. And there probably is nothing more challenging, or demanding of self-mastery, than sight casting to a red. It's hunting and it calls for all of the attributes of a huntress — stealth, acute awareness, sensitivity, quick reflexes, and courage.

The first few feet from the boat I had a big fish chase my fly. I wasn't fast enough to hook him when he nabbed my topwater fly, one that rides on the the surface and makes noise to attract the fish. He got away. And so we proceeded, Scott urging me to follow him to a small cove on the backside of the island. It was devoid of fish. However, Chip on the other hand was into the big ones. So when he called us on the radio about his find, we didn't waste time trudging the half-mile or so through the water to join him.

Along the way, my energy was starting to flag. Wading these waters even with the wind to your back is a great workout. Scott, with his long stride, waded on ahead with my encouragement, and I maintained a pace much easier for my shorter legs, yet casting as I went. I'm not sure what made me stop, but a small swirl caught my attention out of the corner of my left eye. I knew it was too small and too silent for a game fish. Then I caught the sight of a small stingray out of the corner of my right eye. One more step, and I would have been the victim of my greatest fear as a wade fisher. My panic rose, and I froze. I looked at the boat. I was a long way from it, as well as the shore. The little girl in me wanted my husband to come to the rescue. Knowing that this was one fear that I had conquered in the past, it was time to face it again. I took several deep breaths and then a step to the left, and then one forward. The little bugger followed me for about ten steps. Finally, I forgot him and began casting again. By this time though, my enthusiasm for being on the water was waning. I joined Scott and Chip, and cast a few times. Scott headed south, casting along the bank. Chip stayed in place, to my right (north). Then he went to the bank. I followed.

As Chip and I sat on the bank, we talked about his catch for the day. A couple of trout over 16 inches, which meant they were keepers, and a couple of redfish over 28 inches long. *What a day for him!* Legal redfish, keepers, are in the 20 inch to 28 inch slot. Throwbacks are anything over the 28 inches, and it is a big deal when you catch one. Most redfish reeled in range from 22 to 24 inches, or smaller.

So far I'd come up with nada. But I was learning more each time I ventured into the Bay. Someday my experience had to pay off. I knew it. After a few minutes, Scott joined us. We were all tired and thirsty. The boat was a long way away. Chip said he'd buy me a drink at dinner that night if I went to get the boat. I said, let's flip a coin. We all chuckled and started making our way back.

"I'm going to fish back to the boat," Scott said. He looked at me, knowing I wouldn't pass up one last opportunity for the day to perhaps catch my first red. He knows me oh so well. So as Chip proceeded to the boat, Scott and I reentered the water to fish.

I cast a few times, and then changed from my topwater to a small bendback, a fly that sinks below the surface of the water. A couple of casts later, I had a hit. I had had only small success several weeks before bringing in a trout that had just made keeper status. I would have thrown him back except he'd swallowed the hook and was destined to die anyway. This time my rod bent and stayed bent. I couldn't believe it. I chuckled aloud, and Scott turned to look my way. I laughed even louder when I saw that my big catch was an eight-inch trout. As I freed him from the hook, I told him to come back when he was a little older.

Scott saw a pod of redfish coming, and he encouraged me to get in front of him. I told him I'd catch what he missed. He accused me of being on the bank. He was probably right. I had a way of holding myself back, which probably accounted for my lack of fishing success. Scott zeroed in on the leader of the pack. He cast his fly toward the massive wake, and we watched as the fish lunged toward the fly. I held my breath, and after a couple of missed strikes, Scott finally hooked him.

He called out, "This is the biggest red that I have ever hooked on a fly rod."

I kept casting, while Scott played his fish. The little guy that I had released moments before, or his twin, revisited me. I once again told him to come back when he was a little older. I turned and looked at the boat. Chip was stretched out, patiently waiting for us. I was tempted to go back, but my curiosity prompted me to wait until Scott brought in his catch. Twenty minutes had passed. I walked slowly toward him, not wanting to disrupt his concentration nor get in his way. I made intermittent casts as I ventured closer. Something told me this was different than any other fish. After half an hour Scott brought him in. A brief thought that we'd be going to Jim's Pier on the island to weigh the fish in that afternoon crossed my mind, but I quickly dismissed it. It couldn't be a record.

Scott was beaming. "I've got to take this back to the boat to show Chip." I nodded in agreement, knowing that there is something special about showing off your prize, especially among fishers — and brothers. I admit to needing to do the same. When I caught my first red on the spin rod, I had to take it back to the boat to show Scott's father.

I reached down and touched the fish. He was a beauty, with several spots and a scar where he'd probably been hit by a propeller. "Perhaps we should have him mounted," Scott said. I looked up silently. I didn't need to say a thing.

"No, we'll let him go." He looked around. The pod was still swimming in the waters. "I want to fish some more."

"Let me have the fish," I said. "The last time we dragged a fish back to the boat for a photo op he died." Scott nodded. That fish is a sad reminder to us to keep our egos in check.

We do keep fish, when we need them to eat, but we don't fill our freezers. Killing a fish for ego just didn't fit within our philosophy. We've been blessed with being able to live on the

Arroyo, something that seemed like a dream not so long ago. That first summer when I was introduced to South Texas and fell in love, not only with the area but more deeply with Scott, was a magical time. We had numerous wildlife encounters like neither of us had every experienced or heard of. It was a time of give and take, where we offered gifts of food to the coyotes, stingrays, and even the cockroaches. Nature in return blessed us with more than enough fish for our family fish fry prior to our leaving for Virginia.

Spanish Dagger in bloom on Rattlesnake Island

This wonderful specimen of a redfish, or red drum as they're also known, needed to go to the ocean and create more of his kind.

I tied him to my belt and took him to deeper water. There were times when I wondered who was tied to whom. He was a beauty, and his energy demanded respect. His presence was powerful and awe-inspiring. Just having him near me was enough of fishing for a day. I watched him, and talked to him. Occasionally I touched him, feeling his essence and studying his scales, the color on his body and his tail, and counting his spots. Then Scott joined me. I said, "You need to take him now. He's your catch. You show your brother."

And so he did. The fish measured 32½ inches, and probably weighed about 17 pounds since he had an extraordinary girth for his length. Chip chuckled with glee. Then Scott put his catch back in the water, and together we watched in awe as the fish swam away. Scott was blessed with an experience

41

that will only remain in our memories. For this was one day we had no camera on board.

We headed home. I made lunch while the guys had a beer and cleaned fish. Chip headed to our son's room for a nap, and Scott and I scurried around taking care of some work that needed to be done. We had a full day planned, as were most. Fishing was a luxury, and yet it was also part of our job. Scott's reputation as a guide depended on him knowing where to fish. And in two weeks Kingfisher Inn would open its doors for our first clients. There was much to do. That afternoon we had planned a trip to Brownsville to get a load of plants for our yard, which as of then subsisted of a lot of dirt and a few scraggles of grass. That night, we were joining Chip and Sandi for dinner in Mexico.

I came out of the shower and found Scott sitting on the bed. "I think that redfish was a new state record," he said.

"Call Larry," I said. "Don't waste time thinking about it. Just find out."

Our friend Larry owned a fly shop in Port Isabel. He confirmed Scott's worst fears. The fish would have put Scott in the record books, and most likely for years. The fly rod record was less than eight pounds at the time, since the state had only recently instituted the state record program. Once again, Scott didn't claim his prize, a pattern that he'd repeated since childhood. We both groaned, and I silently finished getting ready to leave.

"It was the right decision," I finally said from the bathroom. "It was a good thing, right action. That fish needed to live. He was too beautiful to kill for some record. He's earned his return trip to the ocean."

"You're right," Scott said.

So we continued our day, with the fish filtering into many of our conversations throughout. On our way home from our trip to town to buy plants, we crossed paths with our 18-year-old son.

"Pete, I caught a 32½ inch red today," Scott yelled from the car.

"Did you keep it?"

"No, but if I'd weighed it in, it would have been a new

record. I just didn't think about that."

"Well get back out there," Pete said with genuine encouragement.

"I am, tomorrow morning." We all laughed. We knew Pete would have wanted Scott to keep the prize. His own success at fishing had been pale in comparison, and yet he enjoyed seeing his stepfather succeed, and was always eager to hear of the day's adventure.

We looked in the back seat of our car, the one Pete was driving, and spotted two surf boards. "What's the plan?" I asked. Our favorite question.

"We're going to the Island to surf and then to Bryan's house. I'll call you later."

"Okay, remember the curfew. We'll be with Chip and Sandi. Be safe."

He drove away, and we headed home to unload our plants.

"Is that okay?" Scott said.

"Yeah, he's done that before."

We'd only been living in the Rio Grande Valley for a few months, and our son's driving privileges were constantly being monitored, especially since to get from one place to another meant racking up lots of miles, and on highways that allowed speeds of 60 mph or more on open stretches.

"I really don't have a problem with it. Let's just have a family chat about driving and asking about going places this weekend." Scott has always been an advocate of the family meeting, and we'd gotten out of the habit due to all the distractions of our move and starting the business.

An uneasy pit entered my stomach. I shook it off, chalking it up to my tendency to fret needlessly.

Scott and I hurriedly unpacked the car, and then set off to Weslaco. We had an hour drive, and we were already pushing our time frame. I drove so Scott could rest, since I caught a few winks earlier while he gassed up the boat. He planned on getting an early start for his second chance at the record. I thought of Pete, and prayed that he wouldn't get hurt. His first passion was baseball, and he was set to play in a tournament in a month.

Dinner with Chip and Sandi was pleasant. It was still hard

for me to believe that I was having dinner in Mexico. It seemed so exotic, and yet it was just an hour drive from our home to the little town of Nuevo Progresso. The four of us spent the evening catching up on the news and new adventures. Scott and I thought after moving to the Valley we'd have more time to be with family. I'd been so wrapped up with our building project that I hadn't seen anyone in ages. I barely left the Arroyo more than once a week, and usually only for necessary trips. Visiting, like fishing, seemed like a luxury.

All of us being a little tired, the night ended early, and we were home by 10:00. Scott checked the messages on our voice mail. One was particularly lengthy, and I watched his face, hoping to learn the identity of the caller. "It's Pete. He's upset about some fish trying to bite him while he was surfing."

We both shrugged it off, thinking it was probably a mackerel or something like that. I crawled into bed, and fell asleep while Scott prepared his gear for the next day.

About 12:30 I heard a rap on the bedroom door. It took me a minute to wake up, and then I finally realized it was Pete. I stumbled out of bed, hoping not to disturb Scott.

"I need something for the pain," Pete said.

My eyes widened. Something indeed had happened.

"Didn't you get my message?" he asked.

I nodded, hoping to hide the fact that we didn't take his call seriously.

"I've never been so scared," he said. "I knew something was going to happen today. I could feel it."

I handed him the aspirin and the tube of homeopathic pain cream for bruises. I looked at his side. It was swollen. My stomach churned. We sat on the sofa.

"I thought I was going to die tonight," he said. "All night long I had this feeling that we were being stalked. I even said it to Bryan."

I looked at his face and saw something I had never seen in my son's eyes before. Usually so full of bravado, his encounter had definitely brought him to his knees.

"Bryan and I were the only two surfers out there."

I took a deep breath.

"I saw it coming. A big gray thing, and it hit my side."
My eyes widened even more. My heart beat frantically.
"I hit it back with all my strength and started paddling.
Bryan had to help me to shore. I almost didn't make it. I hurt so
bad." He was in tears now, and I struggled to maintain my
composure. I finally found the courage to ask him what it was,
even though I instinctively knew what he was going to say.

"We went to the surf shop and talked to some guys. They
said it was probably a hammerhead."

A shark! My son had been attacked by a shark. My mind reeled
as I struggled to get my thoughts in order.

My intuition had been developing for many years, and both
of my children had been exposed to the "naturalness" of gut
feelings or hunches.

"Your sixth sense kept you alive tonight. That's your lesson. Remember that feeling."

He nodded. "I need to call Shana." He frequently called his
big sister whenever he felt vulnerable and confused — or was
in a jam.

I hugged him and sent him off to his room. Then I crawled
back into bed. No longer tired, I lay awake for quite awhile
saying my prayers of thankfulness. My son's life had been
spared, and I couldn't express my gratitude enough.

I awoke hours later not even realizing I had fallen asleep.
Scott was getting dressed. He was going back out for another
chance at the state record, even though he realized his chances
of a repeat performance were remote. If luck prevailed he
planned to keep his catch alive and release it after a weigh-in.

"Pete is really hurt. They think it was a hammerhead."

I could see in the dimly lit room that Scott had a look of
astonishment on his face. I followed him to the kitchen, where
we resumed our conversation at the coffee pot.

"Isn't it ironic that the best day of fishing I've ever had in
my life, our son is attacked by a shark?" He knitted his brow.

"Yesterday, I caught the biggest fish I ever have on a fly
rod." He sipped his coffee, and then looked at me. "It's strange,
but the biggest fish I've ever caught on conventional gear was
a hammerhead. Back in Virginia."

I looked out at the water. It was a glassy morning. Perfect for fishing. I thought of the fish that we let go just the morning before.

"The fish god smiled upon us. You let your prize go. Nature blessed us in return. "

Indigenous people frequently pay homage to dolphins, swordfish, seals, red snapper, whales, salmon — and even sharks.

Jeff Zhorne, author of *The Everything Fly-Fishing Book*, wrote "Many fishing families in developing countries still pray to gods of the sea for protection at small private altars before setting out on the water. Often they seek immunity from the shark, which in many societies evokes terror. But for a number of peoples, even those who fear its attack, the shark is respected as a top predator and worshipped for a god."

While fishing in the Caribbean, our friend Cecil told us of several Japanese men praying to a fish god statue before embarking on each day's excursion. They caught fish, and the other guests at the lodge did not, including himself. Although he was a bit skeptical, he decided what the heck, it couldn't hurt, and went through the motions of his own discreet ritual. He was joined by the others in his party, except for one man. That man wound up fishless for the trip, while Cecil and his other companions caught fish.

I really believed that somewhere in the karmic scheme of things, our good deed — letting that big red go — had gone rewarded. I hated to think of what would have happened had Scott claimed his prize. Would the fish god have taken our son?

Scott left in search of the big ones that he'd seen the day before, and I returned to bed hoping to get some more sleep. I lay there wondering if his catch of the day before would reappear. Yesterday's experiences seemed like such a dream. It was the most relaxing day I'd had on the water in quite some time. Seeing Scott bring in that big fish was a magical experience. And yet after seeing a four-inch bruise formed in a straight line across our son's side, I realized that what the fish god giveth, the fish god can also taketh away. I shuddered.

Scott's Record Redfish; 11.94 pounds, 30.5 inches

The pod of fish returned to Rattlesnake Bay that morning. And Scott was given a second chance at catching a record. He called from Jim's Pier, happily relating the story of the second biggest catch of his life on a fly rod, and sheepishly asking that we bring a camera and cash. Scott had caught a new state record, kept it alive for the 15-mile-trip by boat to South Padre Island. He'd carried the fish in a large ice chest, stopping every few miles to freshen the water.

Pete and I watched as he released it unharmed to become a spawning adult in the open Gulf. *What a story!* I marveled at the turn of events as I rode back home with Scott across the Bay in our boat. It was a glorious day. We had a lot to be thankful for.

And Pete? He went off again with his friend Bryan — back into the water, to make his own peace with the fish god.

47

A Matter of Forgiveness

6

September/October 1999. My goal of catching my first red-fish on a fly rod sometimes seemed like an impossible mission. I felt jinxed, unworthy, and untalented. I wondered why I was in the sport. I questioned my ability, and set up an arbitrary standard of my worth: Until I caught a redfish, I would not consider myself an accomplished fly fisher.

It wasn't that I hadn't caught any fish on a fly rod. I just hadn't caught a redfish, my home waters' prime draw. I'd caught small trout blind casting along the Intracoastal Waterway. I'd had tremendous success with small mouth bass on Virginia's Shenadoah River, and I'd lured several rainbows to my fly in the Virginia streams, as well. But the Laguna Madre redfish remained elusive.

The process was slow and arduous. Time after time I'd go out with Scott and come close, but there was always something that didn't quite make the experience all come together. I had many, many frustrating moments. In the summer of 1999, I came very close many times to succeeding at my redfish quest. But there were equally as many times when I almost lay down my fly rod. My ego was definitely being challenged.

One day, we were fishing the flat near Duncan's Channel, several miles south of the mouth of the Arroyo. There were redfish everywhere. Every time I looked over at Scott, his rod was bent. He was a couple hundred yards away from me. Fishing with him didn't mean we were joined at the hip. We often wandered far from one another, close enough to see, close enough to contact by 2-way radio, but not so close that our rods might touch.

He'd caught so many throughout the day, that he didn't even turn around anymore and yell, "hey!" raising his catch high enough for me to see. To make matters worse another guide and his two clients were fishing nearby, and one of the group made his way toward me. It was an embarrassing moment. I had redfish everywhere and was kneeling in the water taking a knot out of my leader. My meager casting ability, coupled with even the light winds of 10 to 15 mph, were a recipe for wind knots in both my leader and tippet. (In our setting, the leader is a 9-foot section of 12-pound monofilament or fluorocarbon tied to the end of the line; tippet is the very end section, measuring 2-3 feet in length, and made of 12-poundmonofilament.)

Finally, I the freed the knots and raised my rod, aiming for a tailing red not twenty feet from me. In doing so, I spooked a red that meandered up to within three feet of me. His alarm sent any red within a hundred feet scurrying to parts unknown. My chances were blown, and I was ready to go home.

After what seemed like an eternity, Scott joined me and we headed back to the boat, which by this time had become just a speck on the horizon.

I said little as we climbed aboard and stowed our gear, but by the time we reached the end of Duncan's Channel and entered the Intracoastal Waterway, tears were flowing down my cheeks. "This is just like my life," I said. "I try so hard and get nowhere." I couldn't admit it aloud, but I considered putting away my fly rod forever.

In reality, my frustration on the water was mirroring the frustration we were having with our house contractor. The promise that we'd be just one month in a rented cottage with our belongings in boat storage had turned into four. I felt like I was being stonewalled at every turn, and I could do nothing about either the contractor or the lack of redfish on the end of my line other than stay with the process. I was too far along to back out of our building project — or to give up fly fishing. I had to see it through to the end, but it certainly wasn't happening quickly enough. I wanted it to be over, but by now, I knew that until I settled into the process, the lessons would continue to drag on.

Finally, we moved into our new home, and I resumed my quest for my first redfish on a fly.

September gave way to October. Scott and I were joined once again by his brother. We headed for Rattlesnake Bay. The action was still hot and heavy. The big reds were still milling about in pretty much the same area as Scott caught his record red. In the fall they form herds and the spawners — any red about 28 inches or larger — make their way to the Gulf. Some return to the Bay, but most are transformed into ocean going vessels.

We got out of the boat and within minutes saw a pod of tailing redfish working the bank of Rattlesnake Island. Scott, in his usual fashion, encouraged me to have the first shot at them. With a shaky hand and a rapidly beating heart, I stealthily waded toward them and got into position. I got close enough to where a thirty foot cast was all that was needed to drop the fly smack dab in the middle of them. It was a topwater fly, Scott's VIP, which at that time was a large deer hair fly with a pair of big eyes, designed to float on top of the water and create noise to attract the fish. I watched as one big red came out of the water. It seemed as if time stopped and I held my breath. I can still see his face and the expression in his eyes, as he broke the surface, touched his fleshy lips to the fly, and then turned away. The pod broke up and moved off.

Scott yelled to me. "What happened?"

"I don't know." I recounted exactly what I did, right down to placing the fly exactly in the middle of the pod, and the fish coming out of the water.

"Did you move the fly?"

I felt my heart sink. "You didn't tell me that I needed to."

I've since learned that when I'm in the process of learning a new technique from Scott — whether it's casting, driving the boat, or a myriad of other tasks — I need to ask specific questions covering all the who, what, when, where, and whys. He's been boating and fishing for so long that it comes naturally to him and often what goes unsaid is what may seem like a logical act or assumption, like stripping the fly (making it move through the water by pulling short sections of the line toward the reel).

The lesson in all of this.... Keep the fly moving. Flies imitate prey. Prey — crabs, shrimp, finger mullet, lugworms — do not lay in wait for their demise. They run like the devil. Keep the fly moving. Twitch that fly, strip that line. Don't let your fly lie dead in the water.

The VIP (Vastly Improved Popper) has gone through many transformative stages since Scott first conceived of the design several years ago. As I've said previously, we like smaller, light-weight flies. Why put yourself through a lot of effort and per-haps misery by throwing a big fly if it's really not necessary, right? This popper is designed to float on top of the water and to make noise, thus drawing the attention of fish from several feet away. This is the latest version that is light-weight, but very effective. We find that white is the color of choice for many fish, but Scott often uses black, red, or orange for the "head" of the fly. The sequins at the end adds a definitive "pop," as you strip the fly through the water.

Captain Scott Sparrow's VIP

Hook: GamaKatsu B10S #4 or #6

1. Tie in six to ten strands of Dupont Lumaflex, sold as Spirit River's Flex-Floss, with a few strands of Krystal Flash

2. Stack one bunch of deer body hair on top of hook, flare and wind forward through hair for ¼" and then con-

---

Terms to Learn

- Flex-Floss is a colorful stretchy material, often used to make wiggly — attention getting — legs on flies.
- Krystal Flash is a sparkly, twisted nylon coming in a wide range of colors.
- Deer body hair is dyed in a variety of colors and is a great material for topwater flies because it sheds water and can be sewn on to the hook, thus creating a thick "buggy" look.
- Closed cell foam is available at arts and crafts stores and insures the fly's buoyancy.

---

tinue winding forward to the eye over bare hook shank. Tie off and cut thread.

3. Prepare head from block of closed cell foam, available at craft stores. Angle both front and back faces, so that block is shorter at bottom to fit remaining hook shank.
4. Push bodkin needle through bottom of block, from back to front.
5. Put drop of cyanocrylic on hook shank.
6. Remove bodkin needle from block, and immediately push block over eye. Move back quickly against deer hair, making a tight seal.
7. Attach doll eyes, or epoxy eyes with cyanocrylic.
8. Optional: slide 10-mm white pearlescent sequin over hook eye, available at craft store. Attach to foam head with cyanocrylic.
9. Cut off bottom of sequin to reopen hook gap.

You can find the materials in fly shops or through various mail order catalogs catering to fly fishers.

One week later, Scott and I were preparing for our next trip out on the Bay. We'd had dinner, and the gear was organized. Scott wandered to the dock to cast to the trout. I glanced at the clock. It was nearing 10:00 and Pete wasn't home yet, nor had he checked in. He was on restriction, due to a serious traffic violation, and able to use the car only for school functions. This night he had to prepare for a senior skit. I checked the clock every few minutes until finally the door opened. One look at his face told me something was wrong. He asked me to step outside. He led me silently to the car where I immediately saw a huge dent in the rear passenger door. In an instant an explosion went off inside of me. It was the straw that broke the camel's back.

In dreams, cars often symbolize the physical body, or yourself. This car was the very one I'd bought after my divorce. It represented the new me, the one that had been freed from years of living far less than an authentic life. My car had everything I wanted on it — a sunroof, cruise control, and a good stereo. I loved driving that car with the sunroof open, the sunshine beaming down on me and the fresh air wafting over me, and the stereo playing loud while I sang along.

But now that symbol was marred, and I felt betrayed, used, and disrespected. History was repeating itself; only the face of the messenger was different. Before I could do nothing about it. My fear of reprisal fed my feelings of hopelessness. I hadn't yet claimed my power to stand up for my boundaries. This time was different. Unfortunately, however, I did not act sooner. I wasn't tough enough when Pete had his first driving violation in Virginia. A second followed shortly after we moved to Texas. My lack of parental backbone led to this final act. The spiritual 2 x 4 was crashing down upon me. I screamed and raged. I cried. The neighbors heard it all.

The next day, after I regained my composure, I did take the keys from Pete, and I removed him from our insurance. To further drive home my message, I told him I would not drive him to school for anything other than baseball practice. A lot of this scene could have been avoided had I taken similar actions after the first infraction. But I felt like it was better late than never to learn this valuable lesson.

In the morning light I was embarrassed at my explosive reaction, and while my son's actions needed to be addressed, I could have made a better presentation. It was a source of much regret. I sat at the breakfast table dressed for fishing, but hardly enthusiastic about our planned outing. But after Pete left for school with a friend, Scott and I headed for the boat and for Rattlesnake Bay once again.

Scott left the boat in his usual speedy fashion. I moved lethargically. I was severely depressed. Healthy boundaries seemed to be the core theme of my spiritual lessons. I paid dearly over the years for not guarding mine more diligently. I was always too forgiving or too fearful to stand up for myself to set good boundaries for my person and property. The dent in the car was a pitiful reminder of this and one that would cost us personally, and at a time we could least afford it. I dragged myself out of the boat and half-heartedly began scanning the water for signs of fish. I walked a few feet, stopping far enough from the boat not to catch it on my backcast.

As I cast, I prayed for my son, for myself, and for understanding of what could make our life better together. I felt as though I'd blown a big test, and I was very ashamed that I aired our family's dirty laundry to our neighbors. I was sorely disappointed not only in Pete, but more so in myself. I was the adult and I quite frankly acted like a raging maniac. Dejected, I went back to the boat and sat, having little energy to fish. I felt like I would truly never learn this valuable lesson about my boundaries nor learn to react calmly in the face of adversity.

Scott called out from 50 yards away. "Why aren't you fishing?" he asked.

I shook my head. "You know."

Throughout my divorce and the nonsensical legal challenges that followed, I had many dark nights of the soul. On one occasion I had to resort to antidepressants to get me through a particular episode. Most of the time, I faced my dark demons head on, and usually came out into the light. I could tell from Scott's expression that he questioned that that would indeed be the case now. I expect nothing from others that I, myself, am not capable of. How could I expect my son to act with dignity and evenness of temper if I couldn't control my own emotions?

Scott continued his plea for me to stop beating myself up, until I finally reentered the water.

As I gathered my gear from the boat, he said, "Hey, God loves you. You did the best you could. Listen..." He was obviously grasping at straws, "if you catch your first red, that will be a sign that God forgives you, right?"

I looked at him warily. He was serious. Always the skeptic, he usually doesn't trust in "signs" from heaven, and regularly chides me for doing so. I often pray for some sign that I'm on the right track. Sometimes they're gentle nudgings other times I receive the spiritual equivalent of a good knock on the noggin.

I smiled for the first time that day, but sarcastically so. Inwardly I thought, "Yeah, right. What are the chances of that happening?"

I turned and walked slowly toward the shoreline, an area referred to as Horsehead, in the northwest corner of Rattlesnake Bay. Within moments, a pod of redfish were tailing and coming toward me. I let out my line. Suddenly I was focused on fishing and not on my difficulties. The distance between the fish and me was diminishing. I cast, and the fly didn't even come close. As the fish continued their advance, I had to lower my profile and in doing so I lost some maneuverability. I cast again. My line tangled. I pulled it back and undid a knot. My hands were shaking and my heart beat rapidly. I could feel Scott waiting with baited breath. It seemed to take an eternity and surprisingly the pod stayed up — that is, they kept tailing. Finally, the knot was freed and I made a cast right in the middle of the pod. This time I remembered to strip the fly. It paid off. I saw a wake behind my fly, saw the fish strike, and felt a strong tug at the line. I stripped the line to set the hook. I was tight, meaning I had a fish on the line. What a feeling!

I could hear Scott yelling, "Keep the rod tip up."

I concentrated on keeping my rod tip up, knowing that if I didn't the fish would surely breakoff. My reel sang as the red took off. My heart pounded.

"Let him run. Don't try to stop him."

I followed Scott's instructions implicitly as I played the fish.

Kathy's first red on a fly

And I began praying again. *Please let me bring this one in.* Excitement took over. I was laughing and crying at the same time. My first redfish was on the end of my line. *Hallelujah!* I could hear Scott hooting and hollering from his vantage point several yards away.

Time stood still. I really have no idea how long it took me to reel the fish in. But soon he was at my knees and I was bending over to pick him up.

"You have no idea what a gift you are to me," I said to him.

He was far from impressive in length, measuring maybe 15 inches or so. But to me he was the biggest and best there was. After taking some pictures, I let the puppy drum go.

Apparently, God had forgiven me. Now it was time to work on forgiving myself.

7

Technical and Practical Necessities

Opinions may vary on the perfect fly on which to catch a redfish or trout, but most fly fishers will agree it takes a certain degree of technique and the right equipment to successfully turn fishing into catching.

Fly casting guru Joan Wulff says, "To get the most out of this sport, you must be independent: capable of choosing your tackle, tying on leader tippets and flies, reading the water, wading safely, and playing the fish with skill."

There is a lot to learn in this sport, and I have — and continue to do so — in gradual steps. However, the following pointers should make your time on the water more enjoyable.

Polaroid sunglasses, which reduce glare on the water and allow you to see through the surface, are a must. Being able to see the fish is perhaps foremost in importance. Without a target to aim for, you'll be doing little more than blind casting, which is not hunting; and therefore does not call for accuracy and precision. It also does not afford you the greatest challenge. Blind casting is an option in some cases, but to me it's boring if you have to do it for hours on end. There is a time and a place for blind casting, but usually off the edge of the channel in areas where you know, or intuit, the fish are milling about.

High-quality Polaroid glasses will increase your chances of seeing fish, and possibly catching them. We use either brown-, copper-, or vermillion-tinted lenses, and secure our glasses to our bodies with a retainer. The wind has been known to whip a pair of glasses off an angler's head when boating from one destination to another. Storing glasses in a pocket isn't advised either. When you bend over to land a fish, no doubt anything that isn't secured will end up on the bottom, and likely not missed until it's too late.

Of course, knowing what you're looking for helps as well. We use object association when describing how to see the redfish in the water. They move much like a submarine. Slow and deliberate, except when they spook and then they're off in a flash. That association is easily imprinted in your mind and so it becomes an automatic response to identify redfish as you're wading the flats. On the east side of the Bay — with its light-colored sandy bottom, the fish tend to appear as dark shadows against the lighter bottom. On the grass, you'll see the coppery color more vividly than in other locales, and occasionally you'll mistake a stingray for a red. The pink of the redfish will show when the sun hits it just right. When tailing, they have a large tail, with a bluish tint outlining it. They wave slowly, like flags. Occasionally you'll get a glimpse of the black dot on its tail.

It's also important to learn to differentiate between body shapes and movement of fish. Most of us have mistaken a mullet or two for redfish and at times even trout. Mullet move like puppy dogs and act a bit frenetic. They have larger heads and slimmer bodies than redfish. Mullet also tail, but their tails are smaller, more pointed, much like a witch's hat, and do indeed wag with the same frequency of a pup's tail. It takes time to train your brain to register a redfish sighting, or to distinguish redfish from a mullet or a sheepshead. Frequently, Scott and I will see just a dimple in the water and know without a doubt that a gamefish is hidden beneath the surface. One cast is all that it takes to prove us right, and our odds are very good. It takes time on the water to become proficient in deciphering these signs.

An interesting observation we've made is that women typically learn to see fish quicker than men. Go girls!

Stealthy wading is important and further allows you to shorten the distance between you and the fish. This means you need to think and act like a heron or an egret. They move slowly and with intention. They key in on their prey and ap-

Wading stealthily near the Trout Bar.

proach them noiselessly. These birds at times become so still that the fish, I presume, must assume they are just part of the environment, like a mangrove or a channel marker. Scott frequently reminds our clients that "it's time to go to zero noise" when stalking tailing reds. If you can hear yourself moving through the water, and if you can see the wakes you create, your presence will be detected. Redfish, and all other fin fish, have a lateral line in their body which helps them detect disturbances in the water — wakes, crunches, or sloshes — that you may make.

A meditative approach is called for, which means you must be focused and you must be in the moment. If you're thinking about the list of chores you need to attend to or the tasks you left piled on your desk at work, you will not be totally aware of your movements, nor completely observant. By bringing your awareness to the task at hand, you will be able to slow yourself down sufficiently to go to zero noise. You will feel each muscle move as you shuffle your feet in the water. You will be in the present moment.

Thich Nhat Hanh, a Buddhist master, says "The present moment is where life can be found, and if you don't arrive there, you miss your appointment with life."

In practical terms, you'll miss your fish.

Being aware of your breathing is the simplest way to come back to the moment. Rapid shallow breathing denotes anxiety. An anxious fisher will not perform optimally. Take a deep breath, and bring it all the way into your belly. Repeat this several times. It'll calm you almost instantly.

Thich Nhat Hanh offers this: "Breathing in, we say 'I have arrived.' Breathing out, we say, 'I am home.'"

Being at home in your body takes effort, and saltwater fly fishing in particular demands athletic ability. The sun and the wind alone tax the body while on the flats. But add to that casting for hours and wading — even on a firm bottom — and your body is in for a fabulous workout. Your reaction to it will depend on the how strong and flexible you are.

I'm far from being as fit as I'd like to be. The condition of my body changes with the seasons and the amount of work I have to do behind my desk. However, because of these fluctuations in not only weight, but also muscle tone and flexibility, I've become aware, sometimes painfully so, of how important it is to be comfortable in my body and to treat its care and well-being as a priority. It makes fishing and anything else I do much more enjoyable.

My exercise routine has varied through the years. At my fittest thus far, I trained with Kris Gebhardt, a personal trainer, twice a week. I also trained a third time on my own and ran four to six miles three times a week. I had a wonderful motive. I was contracted to edit his book, *Body Mastery*, and one of his requirements was that I become intimately knowledgeable about his program.

I no longer have the luxury of a personal trainer, but life at Kingfisher keeps me very active. With a full-blown drought a daily reality, the only way to affordably keep our plants alive is to catch the air conditioning run-off in a large barrel. Carrying buckets of water around the yard twice a day is like working with weights. Hauling gas to the boat does the same. Wading the flats also keeps my legs and buttocks in shape. Pushing the boat compliments my upper-body workout. There is nothing like a little water resistance to tighten flabby muscles. Scott recently said, "We don't have to work out, we just have to work."

While that may be true, a disciplined exercise routine is not only helpful, but necessary for me to face the demands that the Mother Lagoon puts forth. Yoga pulls it all together for me. I do at least twenty minutes of asanas or yoga poses in the morning on days that I'm not on the flats. Yoga not only tones and sculpts my muscles, it energizes me and keeps me flexible, making getting on and off the boat a much easier task.

I also do a short hand-weight routine and either spend 20 minutes on my treadmill or take a six-mile bike ride to round it all out.

Casting from a crouching position

All of this activity is so vitally important because it keeps me aware of my body — how it moves, how it feels — and it keeps me out of my head. Too much thinking will ruin a good cast, and give you a good case of the clumsies faster than a redfish can spook.

Again watch the other fishers nearby — the herons and the egrets. At times they barely move, but when they do it's with intention, precision and grace. So take a break from your fishing and watch a real expert at work. Soak in some of the environment.

Sometimes a low profile is in order as well. Once again, this is where a fit body comes in handy. I've been seen on bended knee more than once while casting to an approaching fish. If nothing more, I bend at the waist and slightly bend my knees hoping I won't be seen. If you can see the fish, they're likely to see you, especially if they're cruising with their heads up, and not tailing with their heads in the sand.

Precision casting is important, and only practice can make you a proficient, accurate caster. Bill Gammel — co-author of *The Essentials of Fly Casting* — is a phenomenal caster and casting instructor. Scott and I had the good fortune to host a casting clinic for the Laguna Madre Fly Fishing Association, our local fly fishing club. We were able to listen to Bill's casting stories for several days, and to take part in the clinic. A member of the board of governors for the Federation of Fly Fishers, Bill sees the subtlest movement of a wrist or a forearm and can analyze what will improve a cast. During his clinic, he asked if anyone played golf. Several hands were raised. He then asked, "Do you go to the range before going out to play?" Several heads nodded.

He emphatically threw his arms up in the air and said, "Then you need to practice before you go out onto the flats. You have the equivalent of Pebble Beach here." For football fans, he also admitted that fishing the Lower Laguna is like going to the Super Bowl. (Hailing from Baytown, Texas, he'd never gotten farther south than Corpus Christi, located about 100 miles north of Arroyo City, on his previous trips.) Once again, I breathed a sigh of relief. I knew it took me a while to catch my first red for a good reason. I just didn't know what I was up against.

But I was doing something right. I did practice. Before we moved to Arroyo City, I cast in our front yard in our well-heeled Virginia Beach neighborhood. The backyard had several trees that prevented me from hiding from the neighbors. Some folks, I'm sure raised their eyebrows, while others stopped and playfully asked me if I'd caught anything. I smiled and politely told them I'd caught a few grass fish.

One benefit of practicing in public is to tame the ego — that part of us who wants to do it perfectly the first time, or not at all, and is embarrassed to admit our limitations. Casting in front of the neighbors was just one way that mine was being humbled.

At Kingfisher, practice is easier. We have a dock and it is socially acceptable to cast on a daily basis. If, for some reason or another I just haven't made it to the flats in a while, I go out and practice. Casting is a great way to unwind after a particularly stressful day. My body seems to need it, like any other form of exercise. I miss the movement when I haven't thrown some line in awhile.

Occasionally I do wander across the street and use a wide stretch of grass to practice without being distracted by rising trout on the Arroyo or encumbered by the dock light and nearby mesquite tree. I see a few rubber necks, but so far no one's stopped to ask if I've caught anything.

This practice has paid off, no matter how silly I may appear at times. Redfish (or any fish for that matter) need to be able to see the fly in order to take it, which means you must get it close enough to them in order to elicit a response from them.

Few first-comers appreciate the importance of a precision cast. A couple of visiting fly fishers were out with our friend, Captain Skipper Ray, and had not caught anything by midday. They asked Skipper if they should change their fly. "Fellows," Skipper replied with dry humor, "the fish haven't even seen your fly yet."

Distance is a factor here on the Lower Laguna Madre. Some days we can make a 30 foot cast and score. On others, our fish will see us and spook 80 feet away.

We always tell people to practice their double haul — a technique for casting a long distance. A 20-foot cast is just not going to produce results. We tell our clients, "Fly fishing the Lower Laguna is like participating in the Olympics." You need to be prepared.

There are many resources available for casting instruction, including videos, books, magazines, and qualified, experienced instructors. I recommend taking advantage of any and all that you can afford. It's worth the time and investment. But here are a few tips that will be helpful to remember.

- For starters, remember a short cast requires a short stroke; a longer cast, a longer stroke. The length of line determines the length of your stroke. It also determines your speed. You will move your rod more quickly when trying to get some line out, but as the length of aerialized line increases, your stroke will moderate.

- Pausing at the end of your backstroke or backcast is important. (Joan Wulff describes this as "a backward-throwing" motion.) Most novices forget the pause, and thus work very hard to get the line to shoot through the rod's guides. The pause allows the line to load the rod. This means that the rod tip bends, collects energy or power, which facilitates the line moving through the guides on the forward cast. Again the length of the line determines the pause: short line, short pause; long line, long pause.

- You may recall the 10 o'clock, 2 o'clock rod stroke described in the movie and book, *A River Runs Through It*. It's a good place to start, but it doesn't work in every situation. Most folks go too far back on their backcast. We encourage people to stop at about 1 o'clock, pausing to let the rod load, and then proceeding with the forward cast.

- The rod stroke is not continuous. You are not imitating a metronome. You need to accelerate to a stop on both the forward and backcasts. It must, however, be a smooth acceleration.

I've worked with former spin rodders, and while the backcast may come off without a hitch, as soon as they move to the forward cast, they forget the rhythm of fly casting and then they heave hoe the rod, only to watch the line collapse a few feet in front of them. Fly rods — and line — are designed to do the work for us. We don't need to make Herculean efforts to cast our lines. We need finesse and grace.

- Keeping your rod moving in the same plane backward and forward is also important. I instruct my clients to imagine slicing through butter on the backcast, and then going through the same slice on the forward cast. It's okay to cast in different planes to reach different areas of the water, but the backward and forward casts should mirror each other as much as possible.

- To learn to lengthen your cast, Bill Gammel suggests commencing with 20 feet of line, and gradually increasing the length of line by a foot until you're handling 30 feet of line in the air comfortably. It's important, however, not to increase the length of line until your cast for the current length is effortless.

- The mistakes will be many, and they will change over time. It's very easy to adopt bad habits, even after casting for many years.

    Phil Gay, member of the FFF Board of Governors, says, "The most common mistakes will be excessive rod motion usually associated with excessive wrist motion, lack of power on the backcast and excessive power on the forward cast, and moving the rod at a constant speed (and usually too fast), just to name a few."

- With that said, seek the advice of a trusted fly fisher in person. If you can learn from your partner, why search further? Scott taught me, but it's an unusual combination. We've seen many women give up in frustration due to the well-meaning advice of their partner. A few times I've had to tame my "New York" side, lest I say something that might offend the more experienced partner.

There are options, and some that don't cost any more than a fly fishing club membership. Many club members are eager to lend assistance to novices. If you have some pocket change to invest in your new sport, go to your local fly shop and pay for instruction.

No multitasking is allowed. Do not walk and cast. This isn't a time to act as if you're checking things off your to-do list. Your cast will usually be inaccurate, and you'll be wasting precious time and opportunities if you do both. If you must shorten the distance between you and the fish, wade, pause, and then cast. But first, assess the situation. Fish are usually on the move. Watch the fish until you have a good idea of his intended path.

Getting into position to intercept a fish's path is important. So there will be times when you do have to go out of your way to hit your target. Wade stealthily to your position, assume a low profile, and cast when the fish comes into range. Casting before the fish is within your range is a waste of effort and may spook the fish. If he is on your "bad wind side," slide sideways left or right to get into an advantageous position for casting. If you're right handed, that means moving to the right of the fish's path if the wind is directly behind you. For lefties, just the opposite.

When sight casting, your presentation will determine your rate of successful hook-ups. A redfish has an inferior mouth, meaning that it's on the bottom of his head. Consequently, the focus of their attention is usually toward the bottom. Nonetheless, topwater flies will bring them to the surface, but only if they can hear it. Placing a fly six feet from the fish will not work, unless the surface is calm. We have seen them charge a fly from ten or more feet away, but only on those blessed glassy mornings.

Occasionally you might be able to place a fly out in front of the fish, and wait for a cruising red to come closer, but this gives the fish time to see you, too. Most often our clients present the fly too far out in front of the fish — or they overshoot them. (This is what happens when you've really gotten your distance up but forget about control.) Redfish need to see the fly as soon as possible. That means it can't be too far out in front of them. It also doesn't help if the fly is trailing behind the fish. That spot on their tail is not a third eye, although they do at times seem to be psychic. It's better to spook them by hitting them on the head with the fly rather than to risk having them never see it.

If the fish is tailing, his head is pointed downward which pushes his tail above the surface of the water. You'll need to present the fly close to the fish in order for him to see it. If the redfish does not react to your fly, he has not seen it. If a redfish sees your fly, he will either take the fly or run from it because it has startled him. So if the fish doesn't show any reaction, reposition the fly closer to the fish.

If the fish is cruising on the surface, and thus giving you a visible target — the v-shaped wake — to cast toward, you will need to intercept the moving fish with your fly. Cast the fly out in front of the fish, about two or three feet, in his path. Let it sink for the count of three, then begin to strip as the fish comes into sighting range of the fly. He'll see it either as it drops into his path, or see it as it begins to move away from him.

- The Fatal Error. Never cast beyond the fish, and then strip the fly across the fish's path. "Ambushing" almost always spooks the fish. You can't outwit a predator by having its prey attack him!

- You need to keep the fly moving. Strip, strip, strip, strip, strip. The prey, a/k/a your fly, should be in the fight or flight mode when gamefish abound. Remember I learned this the hard way. Redfish need a moving target. The fly must act as if it's running for its life. It would be unnatural for a fly to actually move into the path of a redfish and then just sit there. We use steady, short six-inch increments. While it's important to keep the fly moving, don't retrieve it fast. If the fish follows the fly but does not take it, try varying the retrieve.(Strip, strip, pause, for instance.)

- Keep your eye on the fly. I guarantee the minute you take a look at your angling partner, or turn to see what made the noise just to the right or left of you, a fish will strike your fly, and it will likely be the one you were hoping to catch. If you keep your focus, you'll be in the moment, and you won't miss the opportunity.

- Keep the rod tip pointed at the fish, and do not raise it until you actually feel the fish on your line. Most of us react too quickly to the sight of a redfish taking our fly (aquatic buck fever), and we lift the rod tip before the fish is hooked. Your stripping action will set the hook, and when you feel the fish on — don't worry, you will know — then raise your rod.

Everyone has a different opinion on what type of flies work best for redfish. We typically fish with smaller flies that are easy to cast. We use poppers — particularly Scott's "VIP" — the first thing in the morning. With low light conditions making it difficult for the fish to see the fly underwater, the popping noise created by a topwater fly attracts their attention.

We usually change to subsurface flies such as shrimp patterns and bendbacks later in the day. Scott created "The Mother's Day Fly" by tying Lumaflex leggings (colorful, stretchy, break-resistant material) to a shrimp pattern. The Lumaflex allows it to undulate as it's sinking in the water, thus creating an attraction for the fish just in case you haven't started stripping yet. He named it "The Mother's Day Fly" in honor of my catching my biggest red (as of that day) on Mother's Day 2000 using that fly. It was really the best Mother's Day I'd ever had. Pete joined us and made some proud son noises of his mama after seeing my catch. It still didn't encourage him, however, to take up the sport. Perhaps one day.

Here's Scott's recipe for The Mother's Day Fly:

The Mother's Day Fly

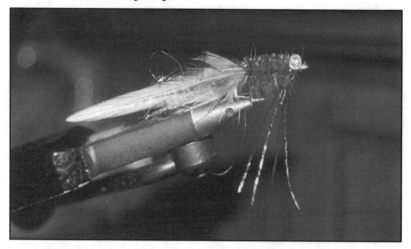

Hook: Tiemco 811S or Mustad 3407 #4

1. Tie in Marabou tuft and few strands of Krystal Flash.
2. Tie in two saddles as tail.
3. Attach Estaz and single saddle hackle.
4. Wrap thread forward and anchor glass eyes, or plastic bead chain eyes.
5. Wrap Estaz and palmer saddle hackle forward.
6. Attach two to four strands of Spirit River's Flex-Floss (Dupont Lumaflex).
7. Tie off.

Terms to Learn

- Marabou is a feather formerly sourced from the Marabou stork. Now domestic white turkeys provide these undeveloped feathers which are then dyed in various colors.
- Krystal Flash is a sparkly twisted nylon coming in a wide range of colors.
- Saddle hackle is taken from the back of a rooster.
- Estaz is a body material made of flashy mylar.

You can find the materials in fly shops or through various mail order catalogs catering to fly fishers.

Colors are also subjective, but we find that red, chartreuse, pink, and white all work well. Scott has a supply of glittery nail polish on hand in gold, red, and silver that he uses when the mood strikes him. (I borrow them on occasion. He's nice enough to share.)

If you're a fly tyer, and enjoy creating your own flies, use your imagination, and let your light show. There are no rules. In fact, Scott recently created a pretty sweet looking Mother's Day Fly using pink and purple. I can't wait to get my hands on it.

We rarely use weighted flies, and then only on the edge of the channel, because we fish in water shallow enough (less than knee deep) that we don't need extra weight on the fly. On occasion though, we'll venture into deeper water and need a weighted fly, such as a Clouser, to get down to where the fish are.

Also, most of our flies are tied a with a weed guard—a small pieces of monofilament tied in alignment with the hook gap— to lessen (notice I said lessen) the likelihood of getting grass on your fly with each cast.

There are several approaches to effective fishing the Lower Laguna Madre: wading, poling and kayaking. As you may have guessed, Scott and I prefer wading the flats to working from the boat. I prefer wading because it allows me to get closer to the fish, plus it eliminates the need to have a really long cast in most venues. Five years into the sport, my distance is comfortably at 70+ feet. I can push it farther if need be, but it is a stretch, especially if I've been casting for a number of hours.

Fishing from the boat allows you to get into areas where wading is greatly impeded by silt, usually those areas along the Intracoastal Waterway and right near the spoil banks. (Kayaks are helpful in these areas as well.) Moving along in the boat also provides you with greater opportunities to see more fish, making it easier to be a believer when you do spot more than an occasional single cruiser. But the fish are also able to see you much easier because of your higher profile. You have only a split second to cast before he decides to seek solitude elsewhere.

Quick reflexes are a must. When you have two objects moving toward each other, the window of opportunity closes quickly. If you're lucky you may get a second chance to cast if he hasn't spooked.

I liken redfish to adolescents. Some days they are warm and embracing and will take anything you put in front of them. Other times, they storm away to the next flat if you so much as look at them. Just don't take it personally with either reds or teens — or at least try not to.

Clothing is an important factor to consider, and the type of clothing you need changes with the season. In the warmer weather, heat, sunshine and wind present the fly fisher with challenges to their day's enjoyment.

There are no shade trees on the LLM, and few fly fishing boats have tops to provide manmade shade. During the summer months, normally we can count on a steady a breeze on the water. However, some days we have very little wind at all. Those calm conditions that we yearn for to enhance our fishing opportunities, then become more of a detriment to our health and well-being.

The right clothing will keep you cool. To protect my light skin from the harsh rays of the sun, I typically wear long-sleeved shirts and long pants made of Supplex. This material is quick drying and highly breathable, and much of it now has an Ultraviolet Protection Factor (UPF) of 30+, as well. There are other materials that do the same. For added protection however, I put sunscreen on all over my body prior to dressing. I also reapply the exposed areas, such as my face, neck, ears, and hands (when I've forgotten my sungloves), each time I go to the boat.

To protect my face, I opt for a wide brim hat or baseball cap. A scarf will add some cover to the neck, an area that I always seem to miss with the sunscreen. An updowner, which is a baseball-style cap, with flaps extending to the shoulders, covers both bases.

Rain gear is a must for every season. You never know when a storm will blow over. It is no fun boating at 30 mph with wet clothes, even if it is 90 degrees.

Winter is one of our favorite times to fish. It was during the Winter of 2000 that our friend and fellow guide, Skipper Ray, taught me how to see trout in the water. However, it was colder than I thought, and I'd failed to put Capilene — a manmade fabric designed to trap heat, but wick away moisture — under my jeans. Even with my waders, my body temperature dropped quickly, and I was aware of becoming mesmerized by the sunlight dancing on the waves. I rallied and returned to the boat, opting to cast from the stationary platform and ward off hypothermia. My lack of proper attire impeded my fishing that day, and I swore I'd be better prepared from then on.

Early winter days rarely call for more than windbreaking jackets and pants for the morning boat ride to the flats. Since the water temperature stays warm to moderate through the first few "blue northers," wading wet in the Lower Laguna Madre doesn't pose a problem. However, as winter progresses and the cold fronts arrive with greater frequency, extra gear is needed to avoid discomfort and hypothermia.

As in all outdoor sports, layering is best, and the number of layers is determined by the weather forecast, and by your own sensitivity to cold. We often face temperatures in the upper 40s in the morning. Couple that with the wind chill created by a 30-mph boat ride, and it can get really unpleasant. But as the day progresses, the temperature often rises into the upper 70s. Just as you may be uncomfortably cold if you underdress in the morning hours, you could become uncomfortably warm later in the day if you can't shed your warmer clothes.

On the coldest days, I start with an insulating layer of lightweight or middleweight long underwear in silk or Capilene on both top and bottom. In contrast to cotton, these materials tend to wick the perspiration away from the skin, thus minimizing the chill due to evaporation.

I wear silk, fleece, or wool-blend socks. Coupled with the neoprene stockingfoots of my breathable waders, my feet stay rather toasty in my flats booties.

My next layer includes my pants, and a Supplex shirt. Fleece wading pants may be an option for those who really can't withstand any amount of coolness against their lower extremities.

Many times I strip down to this layer when I'm fishing aboard the boat and the sun is high, and the breeze is calm.

Breathable waders are next. Neoprene proves to be too heavy, bulky, and warm for this climate. But some protection against the late-winter, chilly water is not only welcome but warranted.

A windblocking fleece jacket or fleece vest is a great insulator against the chilly air. On warmer days, I opt for the vest, because it allows me freer range of motion for those times when I'm able to shed the outer layer — a windproof, rainproof jacket.

Half-finger or fingerless gloves are ideal for line handling. Many times I don't use either. However, boating still calls for full gloves or a warm pocket to keep the tips of your fingers from stiffening.

Since most of your body heat escapes from your head, a hat is also a must. I typically wear my baseball-style cap year round. However, during the winter months, I wear a neck gaiter of silk, Polypropylene, Capilene or fleece. These last three are manmade materials designed to trap body heat, yet wick away moisture so that you don't get chilled when perspiring. I also pull the gaiter up over my head, protecting my ears, nose, and mouth while boating. The windproof hood of my jacket provides extra warmth and protection.

Winter fishing on the LLM can be a lot of fun, and very rewarding. The depth of the water tends to be a lot shallower, so the fish are easier to find. Best of all winter days here often feel just like summer elsewhere. It's only when those northers blow 30 mph north winds that I scurry to find a warm place on the sofa under a blanket and settle in with a good book. I dislike being cold. But when the sun comes out, I'm ready with all my winter gear to go in search for big trout or those fiesty reds.

Adequate sustenance is a must for any athletic activity. Saltwater fly fishing makes unique demands upon the body and you must be prepared or you face some unpleasant experiences.

Having the right amount of liquids and food with you on the Lower Laguna is extremely important. Temperatures in the summer months are typically in the mid-90s. Couple that with bright sunshine and you have two prime factors that could lead to a heat stroke.

It is vital to overlook the inconvenience of having to go to the bathroom in order to keep yourself hydrated. I drink water and sports drinks while on the flats and lots of it. I always have a water bottle with me in my pack. I often wade far from the boat and my thirst comes on fairly soon in the heat of the day. Heat stroke is common among fishers and guides — who spend long days on the water and don't drink enough. According to several doctors who have fished with us, once you've been afflicted, your body will never again be able to adjust to the extreme temperatures, thus putting you at higher risk for repeated incidences.

No one goes hungry here at Kingfisher. Lunches on the water consist of a hefty sandwich, chips, fruit, and cookies for dessert. We also have several granola bars and energy bars for the mid-morning and mid-afternoon snacks.

I'm a grazer, so I eat small amounts of food often. Before leaving the boat on a long wade, I typically put an extra bar designed for athletes in my pack. Calories are quickly burned wading through the water.

Now, back to fishing!

Meeting Grandmother Trout

8

March 2001. A quest for big trout seemed a natural progression of my fly-fishing experience. I'd grown accustomed to seeing redfish, noting their behaviors both on the surface and below, and I even knew what it took to catch them. I was ready to experience a different kind of fish, one that I didn't have to travel far from home to attain.

Like the redfish, and its cousin the black drum, the speckled seatrout, also known as the spotted seatrout, is a member of the croaker family, (Sciaenidae), of which there are 260 species. Unlike the redfish, the speckled trout live in the estuary throughout their entire life cycle. The largest specimens feed in the shallowest water, making trophy trout hunting in the Lower Laguna a pinnacle quest for advanced fly fishers. Four of the current International Game Fish Association (IGFA) class tippet world records have been caught in the Lower Laguna, the only place in the country where you can regularly sight cast to trout over five pounds. Several others are pending, including that of a 37 inch, 15 pound, 6 ounce trout caught by our friend, Bud Rowland. Any trout over 24 inches is considered a real trophy, even though specimens over 30 inches are common. However, Bud's fish, which he released, has everyone talking.

It's been my experience that I will only catch a fish, after I've learned to see them, feel them, and come to know every nuance of their existence. I'm not like some of our clients, who after spending years on mountain streams, head to our place, go out for a few hours, and score on their first attempt. Their path is different. Mine, for reasons yet unknown to me, is to

75

take the long, sometimes arduous, approach, perhaps so that I can share my learning with others, and allow them to take a quicker path to success. I'm not just having experiences, I'm learning to explore every aspect of an experience before it is fully assimilated. I made every mistake in the book when attempting to catch my first redfish. But I learned from them, and now can use that knowledge to help our clients catch their first redfish more quickly. I knew it would be no different with big trout.

Large speckled trout, whose Latin name translates as "starry nebulae" have been Scott's obsession since I've known him. It was part of what drove him south for a six-week writing and spiritual retreat soon after we began dating. I joined him during the last 10-days of his stay, and it was then that my teaching began.

It was our last day of fishing before heading back to Virginia Beach. We were wading off of South Padre Island, barefooted on the firm sandy bottom, in an area we call the white sand. Already a sense of sadness was creeping into my heart. I'd found the home I'd been searching for all my life...and the man with whom I wanted to spend it. He wasn't yet ready to settle completely into the relationship, and I had no idea whether I'd be returning to this place alone or with him. I just knew that I would return. Never had I felt so drawn to an area. It wasn't exactly the feeling of finding paradise. I knew that being in the wildness of South Texas, and in particular on the waters of the Lower Laguna Madre, was going to take me to places within my psyche that I had yet to explore. I stopped fishing and watched Scott cast. His every movement was like a dance. Effortless and smooth, graceful, an art form. I could feel the movement seep under my skin.

Scott hadn't yet scored his big trout in all of his six weeks here. The day was getting late, and finally he hooked up. Scott's son, Ryan, had told me to look for the dot on the redfish tail; his father told me of the bright yellow mouth of the trout. She came out of the water and with it a trail of yellow followed her. I clapped with glee, and Scott looked over at me beaming. He slowly brought her in. Seatrout, or specs as they're also

Speckled Seatrout

called, have paper-thin mouths. They cannot be horsed in, or they'll likely break off. Trout must be played with sensitivity, like a violin. We took photos and let her go. She was big, but wasn't as big as he'd hoped. I took it as a sign of our returning, most likely together.

For the years we've been together, I've tried to understand why he was so driven at the thought of catching a big trout. Try as I might, I really was unable to feel his drive, until one beautiful morning, the first full day of Spring 2001.

Planning to have a slow, leisurely start to our day, we rose at the usual six o'clock hour, sipped our coffee, and then proceeded to meditate. An hour-long meditation before facing the world is our preference. However, now that our business meant meeting people at the break of dawn, an early morning meditation is a luxury. This particular morning I was blessed with a connection so deep that I could barely return to normal consciousness without a concerted effort to become grounded in the mundane activities of gathering gear, feeding the dog, the cats, and the birds, and eating breakfast. In fact, as the day progressed, I realized I hadn't really disengaged from my connection to the Divine. It simply surrounded me like a comfortable sweater.

Since the early days of our relationship, Scott and I have had some incredible meditation experiences, often becoming aware of the same visions and phenomenon almost simultaneously. Before we left Virginia Beach, we began seeing a grid or a web-like pattern overlaying certain images during meditation — such as scenes of our children or loved ones. We'd become aware of certain concepts to consider in our daily lives — ideas that eventually prompted us to make our gigantic leap of faith from Virginia Beach to Arroyo City.

In the deepest states of stillness where "nothing" was visible other than a light background, we often became aware of fine lines woven together, much like the weave on a piece of cloth. Very often this grid was accompanied by vibrations which we felt in various areas in our bodies and which we interpreted as an activation of spiritual potentials.

In addition to personal healing, Scott and I felt there was more to this phenomenon. Specifically, we felt it was related to the Blessed Mother's growing influence in our lives. Indeed, Scott's first experience of the web took place before I met him. He'd been going through a very difficult time, and had awakened in the middle of the night to pray. Upon returning to sleep, he was struck by an intense energy and light. Not sure who or what was behind the influx of energy, he tried to surrender to it, even though it was hard to bear. As he did, he had a vivid vision of a blue cloth in which every thread was clearly defined. As he emerged from the amazing experience, he felt that the blue cloth had been Mary's mantle, and conveyed to him the protection and connection he needed with God to weather the changes that were afoot in his life.

As our relationship developed, the experience of the web became an almost daily meditational phenomenon. In sharing our experiences with close friends, we found that they too had either witnessed this grid phenomenon or had heard of it. One friend of Scott's, Richard, mentioned seeing reference to this matrix in Hindu scriptures. Here it was referred to as the tapestry of light that connects all things in oneness. In essence it is God's web which weaves all of his creations together.

There were many times I found myself cloaked by this web and traveling through a tunnel, feeling very safe and peaceful. This sensation often descended upon me in waking moments, reminding me always of God's love and presence in my life. On this particular day, it was extremely vivid and I did indeed feel connected to everything in my environment.

I entered the kitchen, where Scott was already preparing our breakfast. God or not, big trout were on his mind this particular morning, and he was eager to be out of the house by 9:00. Nudged by his eagerness, I managed to get it all together — my consciousness and my gear — and be in the car by 8:56. I noted the clock on the dash as we headed toward the launch. I wanted credit for my unusual timeliness.

The ride out was spectacular. Magical. I sat next to Scott and tucked my arm through his, grateful for our time together, and having him for my partner for the last four years. While we enjoy fishing with others, the best times are when we go off together. This fishing date was an extension of our anniversary celebration, which included a festive home-cooked dinner of shrimp and pasta that I'd made the night before in honor of our third year of marriage.

The morning light danced on the spoil banks and the water. Birds flew overhead, squawking with delight. Best of all there was little boat traffic. I hadn't been on the Bay in over a week, and the last time I wasn't fishing. I was teaching a nine-year-old the finer points of stealthy wading and fly casting without catching her instructor with a fly. I was grateful for my waders and my ability to duck.

A tugboat pushing a large barge entered the mouth of the Arroyo as we approached the intersection on the ICW. Scott maneuvered around it, then headed north for a few miles before veering east, to a place where I hadn't fished before but Scott had with our friend Fred.

The East Flats of the Laguna Madre, seemingly no matter where you enter them, are extremely beautiful and comprised of shallow, clear water with delightfully firm wading on a

The east flats of the Laguna Madre

sandy bottom. This morning there was an undercurrent of excitement coursing through me. Yet I also remained aware of my continued deep connection to my meditative state, brought easily to the forefront of my consciousness by simply thinking of it. I didn't want it to end. I longed to be able to float through each moment of my day deeply connected to this oneness I felt with God. It took as much practice to remain centered and focused as it did to make a precision cast. In fact, during my tenure as a fly fisher, I was convinced that my mental, emotional, and spiritual state was a direct factor to my fishing experience. If I was off, I was almost assured a frustrating day on the water.

As we skirted the skinny water looking for concentrations of big fish, several times we were startled by large trout as they darted by the boat. Scott groaned with each one. "Did you see that one? Gosh, it was a big one." His boyish enthusiasm was beginning to seep into my own, creating a sense of adventure I hadn't felt in some time. We set down hoping to see more fish showing. Several large wakes, undoubtedly gamefish, were making their way away from our boat. I scanned the horizon. It felt good, but Scott insisted he wanted to go farther east. We did and the fish weren't as prevalent, so we decided to return to our former spot, only to find it occupied by our friend Skipper Ray. Now we were sandwiched between Skipper and his charter, and Fred and his family. I began to feel uncomfortable. I wanted isolation. I wanted nothing to interfere with my sense of inner peace.

I snapped on the Strip 'n Aid, which is a oval-shaped, plate-like device with cone-like "teeth" protruding from the surface designed to catch fly line and prevent it from dragging in the water. This newly designed stripping basket reduces tangling and the need for numerous false casts. It also lengthens the distance of a cast. I won't leave the boat without it.

I headed directly east. Scott, having prepared himself in the same manner, moved northeast. Stingrays were abundant so I slid my feet carefully, watchful for just a slight show of tail in the sandy bottom.

I began casting once I was far enough from Scott and the boat not to catch either. My timing was off, the line was twisting, and my frustration level was rising. Besides that I didn't see any fish in my direction. I longed to be back at our original stopping point. I struggled to maintain a positive attitude and accept my present circumstances. I tried to remind myself that it really didn't matter if I caught a fish. What mattered was that I was away from the house, out of the office, spending quality time with my husband, and enjoying my surroundings. I cast a couple of more times, and decided it was time to ditch this particular rod.

Rod selection can be tough for the beginning fly fisher. Very often we're tempted to go with the cheapest gear we can to enter the sport, only to wind up frustrated. Scott had a nice selection when I started, and since then we've added more to our collection.

It took me quite awhile to figure out what felt right for me. In the five years I've been fly fishing, I've gone through about as many rods. As I've gotten better, and able to feel the subtle differences in rod action, I've become more discerning about what rod I choose to fish with. Right now I'm using a Thomas & Thomas 7-weight Paradigm, and have been for about a year. But that could change if I found something else that really sang to me.

Rods are considered to be either fast or slow action, or combinations thereof. Saltwater rods are typically 9 feet, although some makers have opted for 8.5 or 9.5 feet. There is constant change in the industry, toward lighter, stronger forms of graphite. Selection can be endless. And just like computers and cars, rods will be outdated as soon as you purchase one.

FFF Master Fly Casting Instructor Wanda Taylor says that Type A people usually gravitate toward the fast action rods. Type B folks favor the slower rods. I prefer a slower action rod. This means that the rod bends more easily, and thus takes more time to straighten once you cast your line. Slow rods have a warm, delicate feel, while fast rods are stiffer and more "businesslike." It takes more strength to get the most out of a fast rod, but it does not make them better, only different. I have heard many experts say that the more experience you have, the more easily you can adjust to the requirements of any rod, and bring out the best in it.

When Scott was still relatively inexperienced as a saltwater fly fisher, he bought his second high-end rod. It turned out to be a fast rod, while his first rod had been a slower-action rod. When he cast the new one for the first time, he said it felt dead, like a broomstick. He almost took it back to the store and complained. But then he gradually adjusted to it, only to find that his old rod felt like a noodle! He never seriously used that one again. Since then, he can pick up just about any rod, and cast it well. In recent months, I've discovered the same, and it is very satisfying. Experience will increase your ability to wed yourself to whatever rod you happen to be using, freeing you to perform well regardless of your equipment.

At the beginning, however, I suggest sampling every rod you can get your hands on. Go to fly shops and fly fishing shows. Dealers and shop owners are more than happy to let you test drive a rod if it means a possible sale. And since you're likely to plunk down a good hunk of change for your new rod, you should try it out — not your well-meaning partner. Another tip: Try not to let the price tag affect your evaluation. You may be surprised that a less expensive rod better suits your style.

Whatever rod you choose, make sure the grip feels right. Most rods are made with men in mind and with women's hands being smaller, it'll take considerable effort and possibly some pain and suffering to control a rod if the grip is too large.

As for lines, we use weight-forward floating lines. Because the LLM is a true subtropical fishery with air and water temperatures well above 80 degrees over half the year, we use lines that have stiff coating to prevent them from kinking up in the heat. We attach the 90-foot floating line to at least a hundred yards of Dacron backing, and then we're ready to tackle just about any fish in the shallow estuary.

For leaders, we use either a furled leader made of twisted strands of monofilament, or a standard tapered monofilament leader, usually 9 feet in length. At the end of the leader, we attach a thin piece of mono called the tippet — it's the section to which we attach the fly. Strengths vary, and on a regular day of fishing we use 12-pound tippet, usually about 20-30 inches long. When going for records, we will switch, going down to 8 pound test tippet, meaning that we'll usually have more break-offs, or going up to 16 pound test, guaranteeing most of our gamefish on the Lower Laguna will be brought safely to our feet.

Exchanging my 7-weight (not the T&T I now use) for a 6-weight Fly Logic rod, I opted to head northwest, instead of east. Why I have no idea. I just did because it felt right. I took ten steps from the boat and stopped dead in my tracks. There, not 20 feet from me, was the largest trout I had ever encountered on my own. I'd held Scott's big trout catches before, but

Trout under water

never had I even seen one, much less had an opportunity to cast to one. I felt her watching me; my breathing became rapid and shallow. My heart raced as I stripped out more line and then I delicately raised my rod. I cast once. Too short. She graciously stood her ground. With the next cast, she spooked and was off.

I was mesmerized by my encounter. I'd crossed a threshold that I was beginning to think an impossible feat. My ego would love to have caught a trout big enough to set a women's world record.

But breaking records and winning tournaments was not what fly fishing was about for me, at least not primarily, even if I wanted to engage in a friendly game of competition. A record on the books would have been great for business, and a great marketing angle, but Scott and I realized that records were gifts and given to us only at the precise moments in our fly fishing and spiritual development that fit within God's plan. They were not to be pursued just because it was a good idea, nor to impress others. Our goals had to be organic and fit within the parameters of being good for the soul.

In *Shri Bhagavad Gita*, Lord Krishna reminds Arjuna, "Your right is to action alone, never to its fruits at any time. Never should the fruits of action be your motive."

Fishing solely for the purpose of attaining a record for public acclaim would have been like chasing the fruits. We knew that our path required us be completely focused on the process of fly fishing, without attachment to the outcome of our actions. To do otherwise would surely have surely sealed our fate in failure. We would have been unable to see the finer points of self-development and thus considered the day a loss.

I could not consider this day a loss. It was my day to meet Grandmother Trout, yet another teacher presented to me by the Mother Lagoon. Since most trout over 20 inches are females, I think of big trout as wise women. Here, again the Divine Femine was making an impression upon my life. Even as I cast to her, I knew there was no way I was going to entice her to take my fly. She had more to teach me than could be taught in a cast or two. I unconsciously blew off every piece of advice I'd ever heard from the big trout masters. I didn't move slowly. I didn't let her adjust to my presence — she undoubtedly felt my heart racing. And I didn't avoid eye contact with her as I cast. In six words, I didn't bow to her wisdom.

I continued fishing, hoping to catch up with Scott and tell him of my encounter. He was a hundred yards away, and only a speck on the horizon. He hadn't even seen me casting to her. He'd been engrossed in his own quest. On one level, it didn't matter. There was a part of me that didn't want to speak of it. I didn't want to ruin the specialness of meeting her. Telling my story would be like trying to describe a meditative vision. Words just can't describe some incredible experiences, at least not until they're adequately digested and pondered.

Many of the skills you need to catch redfish can be translated to trout. Stealthy, slow, slow wading is a must. Trout typically lay up in pot holes, and you need to carefully survey each and every one of these areas. Potholes are the lighter, sandy areas in between the grassy areas, and trout just love to become one with their environment here. They often lie right along the edges, and sometimes they will even tuck their heads into the grass, leaving the rest of their body sticking out onto the sandy backdrop. You really have to develop a heightened sense of awareness to notice their presence in these places, and you can do this by moving slowly, and noticing any subtle changes in your surroundings.

Knowing what to look for helps. Again object association is the key. While I liken redfish to submarines, I think of speckled trout as torpedoes, which move with determination and cautious courageousness in the water. They are a beautifully multicolored fish out of the water, but under the surface they tend to appear dark greenish/black. At times, they are almost indiscernible. A slight movement may be the only telltale sign of their presence.

The energy that I associate with a deeply connected meditation reappeared. I waded Zen-like in the water, aware of every movement within my field of experience — fish, stingrays, sea grasses, and change in wind. I refrained from casting as I slowly moved, now to the northeast. I studied every pothole, seeing if she was laying in wait for me.

Dark shadows immediately set my heart to pounding. I wanted so much for Grandmother Trout to reappear. Instead, most were stingrays, buried beneath a thin layer of sand.

In the distance, I could hear Fred and Cyndi talking with their kids. They were unaware of my experience as well, having their hands full with two kids and one dog on their boat. I glanced in Scott's direction, and I saw him crouched low to the water. He cast. I watched, waiting to see the sign of a hook-up. Instead he moved on in his own deliberate movements, stalking his prey very much like a heron.

Time passed and Grandmother Trout reappeared. I could see her clearly. I no longer mistook her presence for anything but what she was. No questioning of my perception. No wondering if the movement beneath the surface was mullet or red-fish. I was now seeing big trout.

This time she was farther away from me, and a little up-wind. She had upped the ante. I rose to the challenge, and took a deep breath. I felt a connection between us. My teacher was enticing me into the trap. I entered with the faith of a disciple as she watched my every movement. I swung my rod back slowly, more sidearm this time than before. I cast, and the wind swept my line aside. Stripping back, I regained my focus and cast again. This time a more precise landing of my fly sent her on her way again. Instead of cursing my failure, I said a prayer of thanksgiving for yet another opportunity to perfect my presentation to big trout.

Presentation is everything. Big trout feed for only two hours each day. So chances are, you're going to be fishing outside that two-hour window. But all is not lost. Scott recently likened big trout to a well-fed cat that plays with a bird and never intends to kill it. For trout, this means that they may respond to a well-presented fly more out of instinct than hunger. However, they will flee from any poorly presented fly — surely more in disgust than in fear.

One day, I was wading with a client on the east side of the Bay in an area we call Grand Bahama with its beautiful, crystal clear water, and firm sandy bottom. We came across a huge trout, which had to measure close to 36 inches. It left us both speechless. This gentleman cast to it several times, and I swear the trout put her snoot up in the air, and said, "Oh c'mon, you got to do better than that," and off she went.

You don't always have to strip with big trout. Trout will often hit a stationary fly. However, you may need to entice them with an erratic retrieve that provokes their aggression. So instead of stripping in a steady, equally measurable movement, try a strip, strip, pause, or some combination thereof. Again, it's important to remember that they are often not hungry, so your approach has to provoke a reaction, not so much appeal to their hunger.

As for flies, we use the same flies for trout as we do for

redfish. Early in the morning we start with poppers (the VIP)—top water flies that skim the surface and make an audible noise to attract the fish's attention. White and black heads seem to be most attractive to big trout, or at least we think so. The Mother's Day Fly is a subsurface hit, and we've of late been knocking the heck out of both redfish and trout with a red and white Lefty's Deceiver. Created by the renowned Lefty Kreh, the deceiver is a simple streamer fly which imitates bait fish. Tied in a variety of colors, it has been proven effective in numerous bodies of water.

At another venue on that Spring 2001 day, Scott was able to land a nice 24-inch trout. A real pretty fish, and yes, another photo op. This time, I did not pose with her, but instead I held her and really studied her while Scott got his cameras ready. She was thrashing about at first, but then I reconnected with my meditative state and told her silently that she was going to be freed. She quieted, and I lightly touched her, careful not to remove the slime from her body. The slime protects the trout from bacterial infections, so it's important to handle them as little as possible prior to release.

She was delightful, and I felt so much love for her presence and such gratefulness for this opportunity to study her closely. It was a truly divine experience. The trout posed with complete aplomb and then headed back to the flats, perhaps never to know how big of an effect she had on me.

Coming into My Own

9

May 2001. We had a break in the action. A welcome relief, despite a slight drop in our income. We'd just been through April. April brought showers, symbolically speaking, that would most likely bear fruit some time in the following year. We hosted Jeffrey Pill's Miracle Production of *Coastal Fly Fishing with Ken Hanley and Friends*. And then just ten days later four staff members of *Southern Living* magazine fished with us.

June loomed ahead. The calendar was brimming over — back-to-back guiding and packages, lodging, visits from friends, and the arrival of our 12-year-old son for his summer visit. He lives with his mother and stepfather in Virginia Beach, so our time together is very special and also very busy. When we aren't with guests, we spend our time with Ryan and participate in activities that are typically more suited to 12-year-old. When I stopped to think of it all, I panicked. It was time to slow down, stay in the moment, and know that I had what it took to meet each of those challenges — providing I had a little time to myself to prepare. It was time for renewal and rejuvenation. It was also time for Scott and me to log some time on the water for our personal fishing.

Our first journey out was a quest for big trout. We rose early and headed to the Trout Bar where the largest trout gather in the spring to spawn. I cast for three hours before I had my first strike. By that time, out of boredom, I was doing my mental laundry list and bam, I missed it. I groaned aloud, and mentally kicked myself for losing my focus. I'd done it again. I'd let my mind wander away from the moment, away from the water and my fishing, and became mentally entrenched in worries about my son and his new puppy, my daughter, our guests, and plane flights for our 12-year-old. As if that wasn't enough to distract me, I was also concerned about the health of my father and my brother, both of whom had undiagnosed masses in various parts of their bodies that needed to be biopsied and most likely removed. I'd taken the focus off of myself and put it onto situations where I could do little other than pray.

It was hard for me to concentrate solely on my own purpose and goals. This tendency was similar to letting my mind wander during meditation. I was so accustomed to multitasking — choreographing people, adhering to schedules, and touching base with loved ones, that I did not know how to turn even a little of that energy on myself. I knew I wasn't alone, but I also knew it wasn't right.

"As women, we are taught to meet everyone else's needs before we nurture ourselves. And as we are groomed into compliant beings, we come to believe that the people in our lives will anticipate and meet our needs as we do theirs," said Jennifer Louden, in *The Woman's Comfort Book*. "When this does not happen, we begin to feel we do not have a right to our needs and desires."

Claiming the right to my own needs was difficult. Self-sacrificing came so easy, and my mother was my greatest model. To do differently in some ways felt like a betrayal of her, and yet I wanted to do it differently. She gives because it gives her great joy. In many situations I give out of guilt and a sense of obligation. I wanted to start training everyone around me that I wasn't always available. I yearned to teach them through my own actions that I had needs that also demanded my attention. With the exception of Scott, I knew that many others in my life wouldn't acknowledge that I too needed to focus more on myself and my personal agenda. I had made myself far too available, and the change would definitely create a ripple in the status quo.

Scott yelled across the water to me, "Don't be timid."

"I'm not timid." I snapped back.

No, just unfocused. It was probably the big one that got away. My record.

My life evolved around other people. Even though our children lived away from our home, I expended a great deal of mental energy concerned about their well-being, their futures, whether they were eating right, what they could do to feel happier, how my son could keep his apartment clean, how I wish my daughter would visit more, and even how I would entertain our younger son upon his arrival. Then there were our guests: Did I turn on the air conditioner? Did I put bottled water in their rooms? When were they arriving? Did I leave the correct key out? Did Bob and Mary eat beef and chicken? Do they expect to keep fish? Will I like them?

Perhaps what weighed heaviest upon me at that moment was my family in New York. I didn't know in my heart if a visit was indeed in order. And I worried a great deal how Scott would manage the Inn, his psychotherapy practice, and guiding if I did have to travel. I was truly torn.

A little part of me whimpered, "What about me?"

I shook my head and came back to the present. I had to stay focused. I wanted to break my own fishing records, and not just the one set by some organization. I wanted to get better at what I was doing. So why was it so hard for me to stay focused on what I wanted?

From reading *Meeting the Madwoman: Empowering the Feminine Spirit* by Linda Schierse Leonard, I knew that if I didn't get control of my "mother of the world" syndrome as my husband calls it, I would go mad. Sometimes my heart is just too big for my own good. I feel the pain of others and want to fix it. I see stray animals along the road and I want to take them home, or at least transport them to the humane society. All distractions from what was truly important in my life.

There was a part of me that knew all of this caring too much wasn't good for me. I knew I had to let those around me figure "it" out on their own, especially if they didn't ask for my assistance. I also was completely aware that I wasn't solely responsible for all the unwanted, discarded animals roaming around South Texas. All of my overconcern impeded any progress toward my goals for true self-expression and self-nurturing. It had to stop, and I had to be the one to choose to make it happen.

From past experience, if I didn't make conscious efforts to reign in my mothering instinct, my subconscious took over. There were times when I did erupt, after giving too much, and having so little time for me, so little focus to express the part of me that had yet come out from under the bushel basket. I've gone through periods where I'd want to run away, find some secluded spot, where I didn't have to care for anyone but myself. It only took a few hours of seclusion or concentrated focus on activities that I enjoyed to tame my madwoman. There were times when I despised her presence within me. When she became unleashed, so did I. I'd cry, rant, rave, throw things. More so in my earlier years than now thankfully. My behavior was embarrassing, so slowly I began paring back unnecessary commitments — anything that distracted from our work at Kingfisher and my writing. The madwoman has never completely disappeared. She remains nearby and makes her presence known every so slightly when my life becomes unbalanced. I've come to view her as a friend, my own personal canary in the mine.

Redfish tailing near a Spoil Island

It was time to move on. Scott walked back to the boat and for the next few moments as he drifted toward me, I continued to cast, knowing full well that my chances for the day were over. Grandmother Trout had graced me with her presence for one brief moment, but she demanded that I honor her by being fully present. I wasn't and she was gone.

We ventured north up the channel and came to a rest along a spoil bank on the west side. We'd seen enough redfish from the boat to warrant stopping, in fact they were tailing a few hundred yards north of us. The wind was to our backs. I bailed out first, seizing the moment. I felt energy boiling within my belly. Truth was, I was mad at myself and determined to do better this time. I was not going to blow another opportunity.

I stayed close to the bank, and Scott moved to my right, toward the channel. I kept my eye on the pod, and my mind and awareness completely on where I was and what I wanted to accomplish. There were about eight visible fish heading our way. I stripped out my line, checked my fly, and took a deep breath. My heart was pounding. No matter how many times I spotted a pod of tailing redfish, I never failed to become excited. I crouched lower as the pod came closer, not wanting one of them to see me and send the bunch packing. I estimated their distance and the length of my casts. They were within my reach at about 60 feet. I cast just in front of them. They moved by. I cast again and again, each time they moved to the right or the left, registering to some degree the disturbance of my fly and line hitting the water. They were now between Scott and me. In the distance I heard boats, and feared that they would pass and send the fish down (meaning they would stop tailing and their presence would be cloaked).

"Cast with me," I called to Scott.

"I don't want to blow your chances," he replied.

"You won't. Let's just alternate casts. One of us has to catch something."

Earlier he caught one small red, which he let go. He had for a time put it on his stringer with the thought of keeping it. Luckily for the fish, the little pup had become as "annoying as Laguna," our dog, and won his freedom.

I made two more casts and then I hooked up. Scott and I both squealed with joy. My reel sang as the red raced toward the channel and fought for his freedom. Scott wielded his camera and snapped a few shots of me playing the fish.

I stayed aware of my surroundings as the fish circled around me. *Watch the line. Let him run. Don't step backwards.* My buddies, the rays, had already picked up my mud trail and I knew one or more was close by. Slowly I reeled the redfish in, alternating my reeling with his running. When he was close enough, I lifted him out of the water, marveling at the beauty of the shimmering colors — copper, blue, gold. We posed for our photo op, and I let him go free.

We typically catch redfish in the 22- to 26-inch range. Legal limits are from 20 to 28 inches. Redfish are also members of the croaker family (Sciaenidae), of which there are 260 species including the spotted sea trout. While both males and females make drumming noises, the male drumming is more audible. Created via their air bladder, the vibration can be felt while they're still in the water, and heard by their podmates. It's often associated with breeding; however, it seems that it might also be a warning device or a cry of alarm to their compadres.

My catch served to boost my spirits. I'd stayed present and hadn't let my mind wander. Sometimes I feared I suffered from an attention deficit disorder. At other times, I believed it was truly a mother's curse to be overly preoccupied with the other people in her life.

In *Faith in the Valley*, Iyanla Vanzant said, "There is a thin line between support and salvation, assistance and rescue. When we love someone or feel responsible to or for them, the line becomes blurred."

I was beginning to discern the difference.

I took a deep breath and scanned the surface for another opportunity. Scott hooked up, and I watched him play his fish, while I continued to cast. Another red brought in and set free. Out of the corner of my eye I saw a disturbance under the surface just to my left. I turned and cast. A hook-up. We were off again, and the adrenaline raced through my veins. I'd turned the day around. I brought my awareness and my attention back to myself.

I was instantly reminded of a quote by Anthony J. D'Angelo, founder of The Collegiate EmPowerment Company and creator of The Inspiration Book Series. He said, "The greatest gift you can give yourself is a little bit of your own attention." He is so right.

I realized how difficult it was for me to focus totally and completely on myself, especially on those things that brought me pleasure. I love to fish. And I love to write. Frequently, I let my obligations, real or perceived, to others prevent me from engaging in activities that nourish my soul. It had been a pattern I was aware of in myself for some time and in which I was trying to rectify. My mother often complained that she had little time to tend to matters around her own home. It bothered me that I had adopted this less desirable trait. She has so many other wonderful attributes, many of which I was grateful to possess.

I was beginning to honor the time I needed to write. Scott was more than encouraging. In fact since we'd been together, he constantly reminded me that I needed to write, or dance, or fish — all those things that I did to nourish my soul. Every now and then, I'd have to have a little fit, more to gain my own attention than anyone else's.

It was getting easier, and in early May I let my friends and family know, that if they didn't hear from me it was because I was in my cave and attending to those activities that were necessary to meet the goals I'd set for my writing. That often meant not meeting a friend for coffee or lunch. Not heading to town to have dinner with my son, and even not calling friends or family from afar until I was darn good and ready. It meant wrestling my guilt into submission and purging my life of unnecessary distractions. I even went so far as to fire many of the clients that came to me for coaching in their writing. Instead of nurturing others and their writing goals, I was nurturing myself and my goals. It felt wonderful and scary at the same time.

Schierse Leonard said, "Identifying a pattern in which you

are living unconsciously is the first step in freeing your feminine energy....Then we must struggle — wrestling with the pain and anger and finding original ways to re-vision and re-create positive uses for that neglected energy in our life."

I was doing just that.

Memorial Day Weekend approached. It had been a week of breaking my own records. On my second trip out, I quickly hooked up. Back-to-back trips with hook-ups and landings. I'd outdone myself. A sense of confidence rose within. It felt good.

We were fishing along the spoils to the north and on the west side of the Bay. Tails emerged again. Two fish later, and I realized I had a chance to go for three. My heart pounded in my chest. I'd never done three fish in one day, barely in three trips. Here was my chance. The fish came closer, I cast. It didn't see my fly. I cast again, a strike. I missed it. I took a deep breath. The fish was getting closer, and I had to crouch close to the water for it not to see me and spook. I cast again, another strike, another miss, and this time it was gone. I couldn't break through my self-imposed glass ceiling. I looked around for a while and realized all of the fish had left the flat. They were aware of our presence and their disappearance signaled that it was time to go home.

Friday arrived. We had a day between charters and I was eager to take advantage of this opportunity to squeeze in one more day of fishing. I wondered if Scott would be up to going out on the water. He was. I ran through the list of chores that had to be done before we left. I put keys out for our guests, ran down the street to feed our neighbors' clan of cats, and in between drank a protein shake. I'd gotten into the habit of getting my clothes, our snacks, and my gear ready the night before so I didn't waste precious morning light and calm winds preparing for the day.

We headed south first, intending to go into Rattlesnake Bay. It was already occupied by a couple of boats and several waders, so our attention was drawn east where a very still, shimmery area of the Bay beckoned to us. We couldn't resist. As we boated over the glassy surface, wakes formed as fish swam away, and muddy disturbances, which we call boils, appeared on the bottom. We stopped. There was little wind and every surface disturbance could be seen for hundreds of yards. We stepped out of the boat, and the water level was above my knees. Too high for tailers, but it looked promising. We knew that reds and trout lurked in the grasses, which was indicated by the shrimp jumping above the surface of the water. This was just one of the telltale signs of the presence of fish we looked for when trying to determine if there are fish in the area.

An effective fisher must learn to read the water and observe the signs of nature for herself. In essence, you need to develop your own intuitive skills and keen eyesight.

Tailing fish are manna from heaven, true gifts from Spirit, much like a burning bush. What more can you ask for? When you see a redfish stick that big red flag out of the water, you know exactly where they are — generally. It might take a moment or two to figure out which way its nose is pointing, but they give you a target to cast to. You must act quickly. You can't count them as good as caught until you see the whites of their big beautiful eyes. They're apt to change direction or move several feet without warning. Any little disturbance will make them disappear.

Trout tail as well. Their tails appear as black triangles, sometimes just a tip of one, cruising through the water. You might mistake a stationary trout tail as a piece of grass or twig in the water. When it comes to big trout, you have maybe one or two casts before the fish will catch wind of your presence. Once again, you must act quickly and with precision. Remember a deep belly-breath helps to bring your awareness completely to the task at hand.

We also keep our eyes peeled for working birds. Terns and gulls frequently fly over tailing pods waiting to scoop up any bait (shrimp, finger mullet, shiners, etc.) fleeing for their lives from the scavenging redfish. Usually a laughing gull hovering near the water is a good sign of redfish feeding. While terns will hover and dive as well, they are often referred to as liar birds because they aren't as reliable as the gulls. It's important to discern the difference between gulls and terns.

Ripples, referred to as nervous water, moving against the grain of waves created by the wind are also an indication gamefish on most occasions. Trust me, with enough practice you will be able to see the disruptive pattern in the water indicating fish swimming toward you. If nothing more, you'll be lulled into an altered state by the miniature waves.

The wake is a wake-up call for you to take notice and prepare to cast. When you see that V-shape created by an object plowing through the water, it usually indicates the large body of a gamefish. Occasionally a very large mullet (a/k/a bait) will throw a big wake as well.

Boils — mud and silt kicked up by gamefish utterly perturbed by your presence, either in boat, kayak, or on foot — is also good sign that you're in the presence of gamefish.

Redfish and trout are, at times, violent feeders, much like teenage boys at the dinner table. They often create audible explosions, referred to as blow-ups, as they attack their prey (unlike mullet which make smaller splashes).

Mullet are one of the food sources for trout and redfish. Where there are mullet, there are usually gamefish. If mullet are seen streaming through an area in large numbers, chances are both trout and redfish will be milling about either under the bait fish in deeper water, or directly behind them. Very often you will see the gamefish chasing bait, sending the smaller fish sprinkling into the air like rain drops. It's a magical sight at night under the lights.

Stingrays form symbiotic relationships with gamefish (or the nearest fisher — you — so remember watch your step). When you see a stingray swimming about, chances are a trout or red will be trailing the ray. Time to put yourself on alert and prepare to cast quickly.

Nature gives us plenty of clues on how, when, and where to find fish. It just takes a little time to develop your knowledge base in order to become a more confident fisher.

Scott moved to my left, and I moved to the right of the boat. I could see fish waking to my right, not the best angle for my cast given the wind was coming from the southeast. But I cast anyway and had a couple of follow-ins.

Scott yelled out, "Hey." He had a hook-up. "It's a trout."

I continued to cast to surface disturbance all around me. Something violently struck my fly and I hooked him. It jumped out of the water and ran furiously away from me.

Scott glanced over while playing his fish. "It's a skipjack."

"What do I do?" I asked, never having caught one before.

"Let him run and hope he doesn't break off."

Kathy holding a ladyfish — her new Texas state record, caught 9-2-02

I'd had hits from skipjack — otherwise known as ladyfish — before, and they've all broken off. They feel like a freight train hitting your line, and usually break off the fly before you can loosen your drag and let them run.

My first encounter with ladyfish was in the clearest water on the east side of the Lower Laguna. We were wading in an area where the redfish were swimming into a flat that was about knee deep with water. We'd see the reds coming from a long way off, and with them, or alternately, there would be schools of ladyfish. My sights were focused on the reds. I made one cast to two reds swimming together and out of the blue, boom, something grabbed my fly and broke off. I yelled over to Scott who surmised that it must have been a ladyfish. I didn't even get to see it.

Most anglers do not want to catch ladyfish because they have an abrasive mouth that destroys flies and wears down the tippet. However, they put up a great fight. When the action gets a little slow, I usually cast into a group hoping for a little entertainment. They like fast moving flies, so if you want to avoid this fine lady of the bay, strip your fly slowly.

You need to remember to check your fly and the tippet after each ladyfish encounter. You'll also need to wipe the slime off your hands, or you'll smell unlike a lady for the rest of the day.

I held on as the fish ran with all his might and made his way well into my backing, which is a thin Dacron line wound onto the reel before the fly line is loaded. Since the thick fly line is only about 90 feet long, the fly fisher needs more line when a big fish heads to the next county. There is usually 100 yards or more of 20-30 pound Dacron backing on a saltwater reel.

I had to remind myself to keep breathing as I reeled in the fish. It seemed like a very long time before the fish was near me. Scott wanted pictures so I kept the fish taught to the line while he snapped shots of the fish in the water. I marveled at his beauty. He was another first, a fact that I could relish now that I'd attained it. I lifted him out of the water and the luminous green cast of his head shimmered in the early morning light. I talked to him as our photo was shot, ensuring him that he would soon be set free and thanking him for this opportunity to get to know him.

I've found that if you talk to fish, they do calm down. I experimented with this one evening. Usually the trout flop all over the place when you place them on the dock to release the hook from their mouths. As I spoke to the fish, calmly reassuring them that they would be released, they then stopped flopping. While I may look a little loony to the neighbors, it relieves some sense of guilt I have for stressing the fish.

With photos done, Scott then helped me pry the fly from the fish's mouth. He'd taken it deep and I prayed that its injury wasn't terminal. It wasn't. One dip in the water and he was off in a flash.

It was time to move, and I took my position on the front of the boat, resting my back against the console. We were heading north and I found myself resting peacefully in the moment and enjoying the beauty of the Laguna Madre. I took a deep breath and a feeling rose within me that was so startling I have yet to say it aloud to anyone, including Scott, who usually hears most, if not all, of my innermost thoughts and feelings.

In that moment I realized that I was truly happy with myself and my life. I was living the life that I've wanted to live for such a long time, but until that moment as I approached my 43rd year of existence on this planet, I hadn't been comfortable — nor accepting — with who I was or who I was becoming. It was an exciting discovery. I particularly enjoyed seeing myself as an accomplished fly fisher.

Scott stopped the boat, and we settled in to having a snack before entering the next venue. The gulls, terns, and herons squawked at us from a nearby spoil bank. Mullet rhythmically splashed in the water, and the wind whispered her secret of life, audible only if you stop long enough to listen.

"You've really arrived," Scott said. "You've got a beautiful cast. You can catch fish. You know what you're doing."

His words were affirmation of the thoughts and feelings that had just swept through my being during our ride.

I smiled, knowing it was something I had to keep within me for awhile. I also knew that this journey was about to have a new beginning. There were more fish to catch, longer casts to make, and more obstacles to overcome. It was an exciting place to be.

Fulfilling Commitments

10

August 2001. Fishing the 63rd Texas International Fishing Tournament (TIFT) was the last thing on my mind. But when Scott suggested I join him and our client on the water for those two days, something in me stirred. I was surprised at my reaction. I had no idea that putting my hat into the ring of one of the oldest fishing tournaments in the country would be even slightly appealing to me. It was.

The tournament capped off a week of relaxation and a change of scenery. We spent a couple days in the Hill Country, where we kayaked the Guadalupe River with our 12-year-old son, Ryan. It was just what the doctor ordered to put some spark back into our lives. Scott and I had been working far too hard, and fishing far too little. I hadn't been on the Bay in over a month. Then we had my daughter Shana with us, and most of my attention was on her. Being an artist, she loves the art form of fly fishing; her cast is beautiful, and she practices night after night on the dock whenever she visits. It paid off. The very first day she went out onto the Bay with a fly rod in hand she caught her first red.

The first fishing day of TIFT arrived. Even though we had to guide a client and our focus would be split between his success and our own, I looked at the next two days as part of my time off, away from the office, away from the phone (for the most part), and out on the water.

I woke up without the alarm at 4:29 a.m. I dashed out of bed and began the day. I was ready, and I was excited. The thought of winning only momentarily danced through my mind. Winning a

Kathy with Shana and her first red

prize was not the issue. My participation was, and while I only understood it intellectually, I figured by the end of the weekend, I'd know why it was so important for me to claim my place amongst the other anglers, particularly the fly fishers.

Scott dropped me off with our kayak at the Trout Bar at 5:50 a.m. He ventured onward with Ron a mile or so up the channel. The kayak was my transportation while I was away from the boat, and also my platform for waiting for the tournament to begin at 7:00. I was grateful to have a place to sit. I knew the day ahead meant long hours on my feet, and knowing our pattern, we'd go where the fish were whether the bottom was firm or not — with or without a client.

I poled my way about 100 yards off the channel, using a hoe handle rather than opting for a traditional kayak paddle. The pole allows us to move through the water easily, much like poling a boat. In this case, however, the pole also serves as an anchor when you put it through the drain hole of the kayak. We have Wilderness System kayaks, both a single and a two-man. Designed for scuba divers, they are incredibly stable. There are times when I will stand on ours and cast as I drift through a section of water.

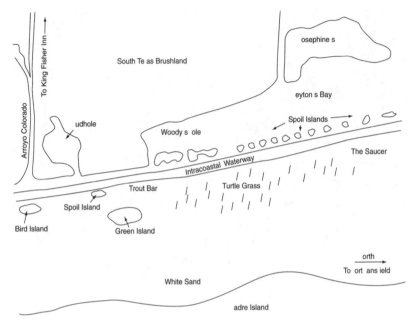

North of the mouth of the Arroyo

I staked my claim on an area where not only big trout were known to mill about, but reds as well. I had one little flashlight with me, but the moon was full. I relied on the manmade source of light only to check the time and for warning the frequently passing boats that the space was occupied. For the moment, I sat in the dark of the morn enjoying the peace.

As I stretched my legs out in front of me and contemplated my surroundings, I wanted to laugh. I've found myself doing more of that lately while observing the circumstances of my life, or in some cases predicaments. I'd suddenly have an overwhelming desire to let loose a really good belly laugh. Like who wrote this script? I wondered. The urge intensified when I imagine the reactions of those witnessing my unabashed freedom of expression. But I held back. I didn't laugh. I allowed it to be a private internal experience.

I believe my desire to laugh was my soul's reaction to finding myself in situations that earlier in my life, I hadn't even been able to imagine — in this case, a lady fly fisher, alone in the middle of the Lower Laguna Madre, perched on a place referred to as the Trout Bar.

I allowed myself a chuckle, and it was sufficient. I hated to interrupt the morning serenade with my self-indulgence. The birds were awakening, and at times, their squawking was almost deafening, but it was uplifting and beautiful just the same. They were celebrating the new day, and I was to be the witness not a participant. I knew it was important to become one with my surroundings and not make any motions or noises which would alert the fish that an intruder was about. With big trout especially, I wanted them to become accustomed to my presence. The catching (or not) of big trout could make or break the tournament.

The sky to the east was becoming brighter, and the moon to the west was quickly falling on the horizon. Soon I was able to distinguish the night sky from the clouds, and I could see that a rain shower was coming. I got out of the kayak and put on my belly pack, my Strip 'n Aid, and my raincoat. It was only a few minutes from seven and I wanted to be ready. The rain came, and harder and longer than I expected. I huddled in the kayak, as the raindrops pelted me. It was actually rather fun, and I wanted to laugh once again, and this time I did, sobered only by the thought of lightning and thunder briefly crossing my mind. I glanced at the spoil bank and determined that I could make it there fairly quickly and hug the ground for safety.

I'm usually not prone to paranoia, but when it comes to Mother Nature I've learned to be aware of what's going on around me in all directions — especially behind me — if there is any chance of inclement weather.

When fly fishing on the flats, optimally you keep the wind to your back, which also means the weather as well. Scott and I love to go out right before a storm. The wind tends to lie down and we're blessed with calm conditions. There is magic in the air. One late fall day we headed out for some pre-storm fishing. In the distance we could see the thunderheads building, but knew we had some time, perhaps hours, before they

Our friends Ken Hanley, Lani Waller and Wanda Taylor hike back to Little Parker Lake durimg the filming of Coastal Fly Fishing.

descended upon our area. We fished for about six hours and made one last stop at Little Parker Lake, which is just down the Arroyo Colorado, four miles from our dock. Big reds were cruising through the lagoon, a place that reminded us of spring creek fishing.

Scott was standing in the middle of Parker, about ten feet from shore. I was on the bank. Both of us were in hot pursuit of our own reds and oblivious to our surroundings. We were definitely in the moment and at one with our environment Suddenly, there was a bright flash, followed almost instantly by a very loud clap of thunder. After a few exclamations of surprise, I dropped my rod and went face down in the sea oxeye and sea purslane, native plants found in the marshy flats of the Lower Laguna. I turned my head ever so slightly and saw that Scott was face down in the water — with his rod in hand! He must have sensed my concern because he soon scrambled to the other side of the lagoon and also stretched out in vegetation. As we lay there unable to communicate with each other, all manner of thoughts went through my head. *"This is going to hurt." "I'll never see my kids again." "A snake is probably going to slither up to me." "I'll probably raise my head and be eye to eye with a bobcat or a coyote."* And *"My rod is definitely too close to me."*

A saying from Edgar Cayce, a well-known psychic from the first half of the 20th century, flitted through my mind. "Why worry, when you can pray." I began praying. I'm guessing that we lay prone for about a half an hour, with many equally bright flashes of lightning and loud crashes of thunder as the first that sent us scurrying. We resumed our fishing when it was over — me, albeit, a bit reluctantly.

When Scott, his brother Chip, and father get together and talk fishing, Howard, the elder of the group, frequently pipes into the conversation with some near-disaster adventure. I just had my first near-miss story to tell, and it wasn't about the "big one that got away."

Being in the present moment not only means being focused, but also being totally aware of your surroundings. It was a scary lesson to learn, but now I'll always check the weather, keep an eye on the sky, and be totally aware of what's going on not only in front of me, but also behind me.

Luckily, this morning I didn't need to run for solid ground. The rain passed and it was time to fish. The plan was for me to have one hour at the Trout Bar while Scott and our client, Ron, fished along the channel near Woody's Hole, a mile or so north of my location. I fished every disturbance in hopes that a trout would be lurking beneath, but none were. To the west a couple of spin fishers were landing fish. I heard one man mention seeing four reds. Our friend Skipper was to the east and slightly south of me. I worried that I might not be doing it right in his eyes. A master fly fisher, he out-fished even the spin and bait fishers two years before, and won the grand champion of the Bay Division in TIFT — a mighty accomplishment.

My intuition told me to head toward the channel. Something was feeding on bait in the deeper water, creating loud explosions in the water. I didn't heed my own advice. Opting instead to listen to the older and wiser among us (my husband), I stayed near the bar, knowing full well that there were no fish there. Somewhere around 8:00 a.m. I heard our boat humming down the Intracoastal. I was grateful; I wanted to go elsewhere. So far, I hadn't depleted the fish population.

The next stop, on the west side of the Bay, was supposed to be our spot for reds, trout, and flounder — all three of which we needed. We all struck out here. I had three flounder bumps, which I remember well from my spin-casting days in Virginia Beach. I just couldn't execute setting the hook. I walked away having caught one 6-inch red and a ladyfish, which didn't count toward the tournament.

The Lower Laguna Madre is divided into the east side and west side by the Intracoastal Waterway. The venues are vastly different, with the east side characteristically identified by firm bottoms covered by either grass or white sand.

The west side, however, can be strikingly beautiful. Grass banks, small spoil islands, remote channels and bird-covered marshes combine to create a richly varied panorama.

There are numerous spoil islands along the ICW, created when the Army Corps of Engineers, the governing body over navigable waterways, created the Intracoastal Waterway in the 1930s. The dredgings were piled into small islands alongside the channel. Over the years, these spoil islands have eroded, and spilled silt into the west side of the lagoon. Because of this, the west side is difficult to wade in some places, and the clarity of the water can deteriorate in high winds. But the soft-bottom conditions also create habitat for shrimp and crabs, which in turn attract reds and trout. The west side can be one of the most exciting places to fish. Only there will you find pods and schools of tailing redfish feeding on shrimp, with terns and gulls hovering overhead. This occurs mostly in the spring and fall, in the early morning and early evening hours, and can provide fast and furious action.

We headed north and stopped along the channel by the dredging levy, a containment for the dredge spoils which is now required to prevent the silt from washing back into the Intracoastal. Scott suggested I stay outside and fish the flat along the ICW. He and Ron walked across the spoil into an area known as Peyton's Bay. He was going to radio me if it looked good. However, the radios didn't work because we were too far apart. There were reds milling about the bank, with their backs out of the water; and no matter how many times he yelled I did not hear him.

To top it off, I was distracted by a storm looming in the east. Thunder boomed, sending a chill up my spine. I heard my mother's voice in my head. While she has a big heart, she always expects the worst and is always warning those she loves against impending doom. I've inherited this trait as well. For years, I've been purging this psychic distraction from my consciousness. I've succeeded in peeling away many of the layers, but have yet to get to the core, which was now showing itself.

I surveyed my options. Go to the boat and huddle beneath the kayak (which was now strapped to the top of the boat) — or head to the spoil and lay up close against the bank by the levy. I didn't like either option.

My heart pounded, and my mind whirled. I couldn't focus, and I couldn't fish. I silently asked, "Am I going to die?"

A wise voice answered, "Not today, Kathleen."

I know when I'm called by my proper name I better listen. But still I could not get comfortable. Boats were running to the south at full throttle, or so it seemed. Some fishers were taking refuge on the fishing shacks along the ICW. These structures — some crude, others quite elaborate — are permitted through Texas Parks and Wildlife. They are privately owned, though no one seems to mind if a stranded fisher seeks shelter on occasion.

I went back to the boat, put on my rain gear and stowed my rod. I trudged through 200 feet of water, praying not to step on a stingray. My intent was to plead with Scott to make the run south.

Breathless, I made it to the far bank and yelled out to him. "The storm, there's lightning, and everyone's running south."

"It'll play out. I'm fishing."

I heard the tone in his voice, which meant, we weren't moving and he wasn't going to stop fishing. I stood there a moment feeling frustrated and angry, but not at him, at myself. I broke my cardinal rule: *Don't let fear rule your life.* I too could have been fishing.

Carl Jung said, "One does not become enlightened by imagining figures of light but by making the darkness conscious."

I felt like someone, most likely my Self, with a big S meaning my soul, was shining a spotlight at the nooks and crannies in my ego self that still harbored my fear. The only consolation was my firm belief that if it was being brought to my consciousness, it was being squeezed out of me, perhaps for good this time.

I wondered how many opportunities I missed once again because of my foolishness. I walked back across the spoil, back to the boat (the storm did indeed look like it was playing out), and grabbed my rod and a sandwich. I trudged back across the flat. I wasted an hour of valuable fishing time, which I'm sure contributed to my eventual fishless day.

I did have opportunities at this venue. The first one appeared as soon as I set foot into the water after crossing the spoil. A coppery back making its way down the bank made my heart leap; this time with excitement, not fear. I crouched low to the water. He was dangerously close, and could easily see me. He was also upwind. I weighed the option of waiting for him to pass or make the backcast. Against my intuition (once again) I made a backcast, the fly landed on his head, and he spooked. I damned myself for not being patient. Chances are he would have gone right on by me and I could have made an easier cast, with the wind to my advantage — and probably caught my fish.

I realize anglers speculate a lot. If only we'd gone here, if only I'd used a topwater fly, if only I'd taken my shot sooner...For me, it's endless. Scott's mentioned he's never seen someone so intent on personal mastery and so willing to take feedback (a/k/a constructive criticism). I ruthlessly examine every situation, especially those where I've "failed," to determine if I could have responded more appropriately. Darla, my spiritual mentor, often reminds me that I'm guilty of beating myself up, which only perpetuates my sense of failure. The truth is if I've done something to hurt someone, I want to make amends if at all possible. Ultimately, I want to make sure I don't repeat my mistakes. Unfortunately, enlightenment is a long way off yet, and I often find myself in similar situations, which provide me with ample opportunities to respond more appropriately. I do see improvement, especially on the water where the Mother Lagoon provides me with never-ending scenarios to "get it right."

Later that day while Scott and I were on our way to the weigh-in, I confessed my errors. I didn't want, nor need, to have him point out the time I wasted worrying about my imagined death by lightning bolt. Nor did I need to be reminded that had I trusted my own internal wisdom and fished the channel along the Trout Bar, I most likely would have caught fish.

Fear had always been my biggest enemy. And after finding the courage to make some major life changes — and thriving not only surviving — I vowed I would never let fear control my life again. But still I had to keep it at bay with constant vigilance.

In *Courage and Contentment*, Gurumayi Chidvilasananda said, "When you decide once and for all that you will not allow adversities to overwhelm you or dictate your opinion of yourself and the rest of the world, you will feel lighter. You will feel glorious."

I did. The weight had been lifted. I knew that feeling, and I liked it. I wasted years locked in an imaginary prison; years that I cannot get back. Hard lessons learned. I could have learned them more quickly, if I had listened to my own inner promptings. It remains an ongoing battle. However, the doubt comes less frequently and with less intensity.

Thankfully, on this day it was just an hour. I was able to break through that fearful voice, and listen to the One that I knew I could trust completely; the One that I follow more often than not. This voice confirmed the rightness of entering this contest, and convinced me that I must, and that somewhere in the divine order of the universe there were fish out there that agreed to work with me and teach me what I needed to know and needed to learn — even if it meant giving their lives to do so.

I knew that this experience was about owning something so deep and sacred in my own psyche, that I must do it, or die. Perhaps not literally, but soulfully, which is far worse than a physical death. I'd come close to that death before, and I didn't ever want to go there again. Anyone can go through the motions of life, but if we live without authenticity, without passion, what good is this life that we've been given anyway?

Sarah Ban Breathnach reminded us in *Simple Abundance: A Day of Comfort and Joy*, that "Each of us possesses an exquisite, extraordinary gift: the opportunity to give expression to Divinity on earth through our everyday lives."

But to do that, our hearts must be fully engaged in all that we do. Only then are we following an authentic path, and being true channels for God's love.

Scott joined the line for the weigh-in, while Sam, our 4-month-old lab, and I sat in the stands. Our client had a small trout of about 18 inches to weigh-in as well. I kept my ears perked for other angling stories. So far I heard no other fly fishing results. One of our guests at the Inn had a 26-plus-inch red to weigh-in. Mostly, I heard that the fishing was tough. I knew that wasn't my problem.

"Skipper defected," Scott relayed upon his return. This meant that Skipper left his fly rod at home and was spin fishing.

A hint of relief fluttered to the surface of my consciousness. I realized that I still considered having a chance at placing in the fly division, despite my poor standing after the first day — with the knowledge that fishing was tough for others and now some of the best anglers were opting for other means of winning the contest. Once again this silent confession startled me. As I witnessed my thoughts, not only did I acknowledge my competitive edge, but also I wasn't beating myself up. I heard myself affirm that I was a good fly fisher, and I knew I could have done better. We got up to leave, while I pondered what I needed to do the next day.

As we drove along the road near the Refuge, Scott roused me out of my thoughts. "You don't have to fish tomorrow. You can stay home and rest."

I considered his suggestion briefly. It took only moments to process what staying home would mean to my spiritual unfoldment. I'd been struggling with a pattern of not committing myself fully to my experiences, of not going all the way into my choices, of always backing out right before I would most likely achieve success, or not doing what I needed to do to attain a goal I'd said I wanted.

Early in my writing career, I received an assignment from a national magazine. I never did the story. After several rejections from publishers for my novel, I turned my attention to other projects (mainly other people's projects) leaving it stuffed in a box in the closet, at least until recently. Even in fly fishing, I never took the time to study what I needed to in order to pass the FFF casting instructors exam when I had the prime opportunity to take it. I held back. It was a lifelong pattern and I was, to be quite frank, sick of it.

"I'm fishing. I need to go through with this."

Mission Accomplished

The next morning came quickly, and I was slow to rise. Scott got up first and shut off the alarm. I stumbled into the bathroom feeling every aching muscle and joint scream out at me. I'd not been attending to my body the way I should for the last month or so, and I was paying for it. There's one thing about the Bay: If you're not in shape when you step foot into her, you will be. Despite my groaning, I secretly reveled in my tighter muscles, and vowed to do what I needed to do to get back to where I wanted to be physically.

Just moments before 6:00, Ron arrived and the three of us meandered to the boat. The plan was to stay together. We boated north and disembarked along the Intracoastal at the third pass into the West Bay. Ron and I dropped Scott off first, and then putted just a hundred yards north. I stopped the boat and readied for the day. Bait crashed violently just a few feet from the boat, which meant there was fish feeding. Ron and I scurried out and assumed our places. It was starting time for day two of the tournament.

My heart pounded with excitement as I threw my fly into the boiling mass of fish. I missed several strikes and cursed aloud my poor response. Then I began catching one ladyfish after another. I cursed them as well. Any other day, I'd delight in the play they provided — the leaping, running, and finally the landing. But not this day. They were a distraction, and they stole my flies from near my intended targets — in this case, trout.

I brought one ladyfish in with the fly deep in the gullet. I looked down at my hands and my shirt, and they were cov-

Kathy playing a fish in the mudhole.

ered with blood. I tried for several minutes to release the fly before realizing my attempts were in vain. I cut the fly loose and let the fish go, knowing it was going to die. My stomach tightened and I fought the urge to vomit. A silent prayer for the ladyfish was the only thing that brought me back to the task at hand and settled my queasy stomach.

After tying on a new fly, I reflected upon my attempts to save the ladyfish. I knew moments after landing it, that it wouldn't make it. But I tried to bring it back to life, despite knowing the futility of my actions. It made me think of Shana. I spent the last few waking moments of the evening before listening to her bemoan the fact that her current male interest just wasn't willing to make things work. It'd been a theme we'd discussed for the last few months. It's hard enough to listen to a friend repeatedly expound on the hopelessness of a love situation; it's worse when it's your daughter. I wanted to shake her. *Wake up; don't be like I was.*

Women have an innate tendency to commit endless time and energy into hopeless situations. We have a deep, unconscious desire to be martyrs for better or worse. Often we go against our better judgment to make things work, be it in a relationship or a job, or even a friendship. I've done this time and time again. Did I not continue to fish the Trout Bar earlier the day before, instead of fishing along the channel? Did I actually think I could make the fish appear by staying a little longer along the bar?

The ladyfish action continued, and I persisted in cussing. After countless ladyfish, I knew my attitude needed an adjustment. I'd just keep catching ladyfish until I accepted my present circumstances. Resistance only perpetuates our unpleasantries and preents us from entering the divine flow of life.

There is a system of mindfulness techniques called the "kriyas of integration," which when applied initiate changes in the mind, body, and spirit simultaneously. I first learned of them when I was in a breathwork training course. Breathwork is a therapeutic healing tool designed to dismantle the unhealthy restrictive patterns of breathing that develop due to injury and stress. A yoga-based healing art, often referred to as pranayama, its assists us in returning our breath to its natural rhythm; thereby, we are able to balance our emotions and enhance our physical health.

Acceptance is one of the kriyas. Over the years I've tried to will away aggravating situations, many involving relationships with loved ones or clients. However, change only came about when I accepted the situation, and no longer viewed myself as a victim, a position I often felt justified in declaring in many circumstances. By claiming my power and freeing the energy it took to focus on the problem, I was usually able to see the situation differently. In many cases, my difficulties magically disappeared.

A large ladyfish jumped on my fly and took off. It ran for the channel, and ran deep. My reel sang, and I allowed myself to enjoy the play. It was a lot of fun. I brought in a 20-plus-inch ladyfish, which I promptly released. Skipper informed me the next day at lunch that it was most likely a new state record, which he currently held. (I did go onto break his record on September 2, 2002, when I landed a 3.1 pound, 24½ inch ladyfish.)

I then began catching trout. It had been so long since I had a large trout on the end of my line. We often caught undersized ones on the dock at night, which is a lot of fun, and good casting practice. But today, I really was hoping to catch something big, and possibly even the new IGFA world's record for women. The IGFA women's saltwater records had been established on January 1, 1998, and many of the fly rod records had yet to be established, or could easily be broken with a sizable fish.

Rumor had it that one of my sister anglers was angling for her own record. It upped the ante. I wasn't just competing against a number on a record book. There was a real person after the same goal. This knowledge was what I needed to hold my feet to the fire and also to evaluate the importance of this personal agenda. I needed to get serious in my pursuit. If a goal, such as setting a new record, wasn't important then why should I waste time pursuing big trout? Why not just fish for fun? Why then is this tournament so important?

Outside of the external validation, which would only be temporary, I knew that fly rod competition, being it the TIFT or the pursuit of women's world record for sea trout, would provide me with the base from which to grow beyond my current level of expertise. I yearned to be a better caster, and to catch not only more fish, but the older wiser ones as well. I also longed to be wiser and more efficient in my execution of life's challenges. The Bay was my practice ground, a mirror for those bigger events in my life.

Catskill mountain fly-fishing legend Edward R. Hewitt once said, "First a man tries to catch the most fish, then the largest fish, and finally the most difficult fish."

The same can be said for women. At this stage of my fly-fishing career, trout were the most difficult ones.

Two hours of trout action passed. Scott caught several 16- to 20-inch fish, and kept one. I had two on my stringer, the

Redfish

Kathy about to land a fish.

first one coming in at 17, and the next at 18. I released several others that were smaller. Ron reeled in eighteen trout, many of which he set free, and numerous ladyfish. He was beaming.

We boarded the boat, satisfied with our early morning success. We boated north to the levy once again. It was 9:30 a.m. when we crossed the spoil. We fished for about an hour, with meager results. At one point, I was standing 200 yards from shore and I said a brief prayer: "I need a 25 inch red or better." Out of the corner of my eye, not 20 feet from me, a large tail popped out of the water. I cast to it and it disappeared. I'm reminded that as Jesus proclaimed in Matthew 21:22: "And all things, whatever ye shall ask in prayer, believing ye shall receive."

I realized I should have prayed for catching the fish, not just seeing it. The fish did appear, but not at the end of my line.

In *Sacred Encounters with Mary*, my husband Scott wrote, "Through such passionate prayers, we expose our vulnerabilities, and by doing so we finally enter a relationship where we become fully revealed — which may be the point at which the Divine can, in turn, become more fully revealed to us."

Over the years, I've become better at revealing myself to God, and making my desires known. I have asked for specific — often mundane — items, such as a new car and the perfect outfit to wear to a holiday party, and received them. Of late, it's become less important to ask for certain things, other than the health and safety of myself and loved ones. I've learned to surrender my will to the will of the Divine. It has made for a more personal relationship not only with the masculine image of god, but the feminine as well.

In regard to this idea, C. S. Lewis said, "By unveiling, by confessing our sins, by 'making known' our requests, we assume the high rank of persons before Him. And He, descending, becomes a person to us."

With little success, we decided to leave. We ran south and then entered the second pass of Peyton's Bay. We boated along seeing redfish darting here and there. The plan was to pole along the bank with the wind to our favor. But as we were passing over a particularly shallow part of the lagoon, the heat alarm on the motor went off and Scott had no choice but to shut down. We came to a sudden halt in five inches of water. Our plan had been abruptly changed. He cursed, fearing that our plight would dash our hopes for success. I wanted to offer some profound advice, but one look at his face, and I thought better of it.

"I can get up by those two duck blinds," he said, trying to put the best spin on the situation and pointing to another cut in the spoils more than a mile away. The Bay provides duck hunters with a bevy of opportunities in the fall and winter. Frequently the remnants of their hideouts, pieces of wood covered with palm fronds, are left behind. "You two start walking that way — and fish," he added.

Aye, aye Captain. I grabbed a sandwich, as did Ron. We started walking, thinking at first that our chances to catch fish were nil. I realized that instead of aiming straight toward the shore of the spoil we needed to head north and then cut across when we were closer to the blinds. If we didn't we'd be casting directly into the wind and miss any fish that might cross our path. I prompted Ron to do so, and I swung to his right and did the same. We were soon surprised to see that there were redfish cruising nearby. We quickly became serious about fishing. Apparently the captain's error had landed us in a golden opportunity. Ron cast vigorously to several fish, as did I. We both missed.

I glanced at Scott and saw that he hooked up. While pushing the boat, he had pulled out his rod and kept it within reach so that he could cast when opportunity presented itself. I was relieved that he was doing more than playing boat slave.

Then Ron yelled to me. A fish was out of his reach and swimming my way from left to right. He was cruising at a good clip, and I knew he'd be upwind of me before long. By the time I got into position and cast, he was. The line came back at me like a wet noodle. To make matters worse, he was now veering toward me. I crouched low to the water, knowing that if I didn't the fish would see me. I cast again, with the same results. I yelled out loud, thinking of God: "I could use a little help here."

Time slowed down and every movement seemed to be in freeze frame. I knelt, and cast into the wind. The line audibly shot through the guides on my rod. The fly landed a short distance from the fish, between us. The fish spied the fly. I held my breath, hoping he wouldn't take his eyes off of the fly and spy me in doing so. I stripped feverishly, remembering to keep my fly moving, and then came the strike. As the fish turned and ran, I rose to my feet, vaguely aware that Ron had been watching this entire act. I began to breathe again, and for a moment considered yelling to Scott, but didn't. I knew that if I did, I'd most likely break off. *I must stay focused on myself.*

I let him run, knowing that he wasn't as big as the 25-inch red I'd prayed for, but I knew he was a red, and I bet he was over 20. I landed him, breathless. My knees were weak and shaking. This fish was nothing less than a miracle. The line shot like a bullet out of my rod, and the fish behaved predictably, allowing me to use my skill to bring him in. I was graced with this catch. I thanked him, and then put him on the stringer.

In *A River Runs Through It*, Norman MacLean wrote: "All good things come by grace, and grace come by art, and art does not come easy."

This art form, fly fishing, was not coming easy. But I was getting better at it because of all my efforts. Thus, this allowed grace to meet me part way.

I knew in my heart that I'd caught my share. I couldn't ask for anything other than that. This tournament wasn't about winning for me. That was over the day before. It was about going fully into my experience and delighting in the dance of sighting, stalking, and catching fish.

Sometimes keeping fish is equally important. Releasing or keeping fish is a difficult subject for many fly fishers, and as a fish-eating vegetarian, it is one I've pondered time and time again. While most fly fishers are not meat fishermen and not intent on filling the freezer, Scott and I do keep some fish, as do most of our clients. A firm catch-and-release policy is difficult for us to institute for our clients or ourselves. There are fly fishing destinations that not only advocate catch and release of all fish, but also demand it. In fact, you most likely will be required to pinch down the barb on your flies to fish these locales, which are mostly freshwater venues.

I did not keep the first few fish I caught, but I was eating those that Scott caught and kept. Suddenly, I realized in order to really claim my experience I needed to put fish in the cooler as well. It was not easy, but it also wasn't responsible of me to expect Scott to be the only one to put the fish on the table. If we're going to eat them, we've agreed that we have to be willing to kill them.

In *I Don't Know Why I Swallowed the Fly*, which was the first fly fishing book written by a woman I ever read, Jessica Maxwell wrote, "Death is big. Taking the life of anything is a very big deal indeed. The first time I caught a salmon I asked my fishing guide to let me kill it myself, because I knew I had to. So I raised his battered, bloodstained fish club and smacked the seventeen-pound chinook right on its beautiful silver-and-blue head. My aim was true. My fish died with a heart-stopping quiver. And I burst into tears...It is a far more honest place...."

I'm not doing my best as a human being if I'm not being honest, either with myself or others. Sometimes this means I have to kill fish, even though it gets harder as time goes by. I'm eating a lot more soybeans than fish these days.

So how do I do it? I pray, and I ask if the soul of the fish is in agreement with my keeping it. I can honestly say I do know when to keep a fish and when to let them go.

In *Creations Heartbeat*, Linda Schierse Leonard described the intimate relationship that the nomadic tribes of Siberia, Lapland, and Alaska have with the reindeer, which they rely upon for clothing and food. These peoples don't look upon the reindeer as mere sustenance. They believe that the reindeer are to be revered; they are "messengers between heaven and earth, bridges between spirit and nature." She wrote, "Yielding to Nature, rather than confronting or controlling it, is a major part of the art of hunting. Moving with the environment, not mastering it, is the essential moral and spiritual attitude that honors the ancient agreement with the animals who offer themselves to the hunter."

Fly fishing on the shallow flats of the Lower Laguna Madre is hunting. Yet I do not look upon the redfish or trout that I put

Kathy embracing one of her friends.

on my table with disdain. I am deeply connected to each and every one, which is why it is often so difficult to take even one life. But as Schierse Leonard explained, I really believe on this day the fish I caught made an agreement with me on a deep spiritual level. Sometimes it's important to honor that agreement, to make the kill.

In May of 2000, my parents visited. When we weren't caught up in my son's graduation festivities, my father fished. He fished at night and he fished in the morning. It's in our blood. I enjoyed seeing him spend time on the dock waiting for the fish to bite. He throws bait, jigs, and gold spoons, not having followed in his daughter's footsteps.

One morning I was sitting in my office, trying to catch up on the endless paperwork that comes with running a business and a household. I'd been busy with family activities for more than a week. In part, I was hiding. I need a certain amount of solitude in order to function. If not, I dissociate, which isn't conducive to being present, nor enjoying the flow of life.

Dad came rushing through the back door. "I think I caught a keeper. How big does it have to be?" he asked, holding the fish up for me to see.

I barely raised my eyes from the computer. "Not sure, Dad. Better throw it back."

I didn't even get up to witness his catch or to search the *Texas Parks and Wildlife Outdoor Annual* for the size limits. To this day, it's something I regret. I wasn't present for him. And in looking back I wasn't present for myself. I couldn't allow myself to enjoy the last few days of his visit to the fullest. I confessed my regret to him in a letter after he returned home. In his delightful wisdom, he said he didn't need to keep fish; he'd done that plenty. But I feel like it might have been important for him to keep that one, on that day. A mere picture might have been nice.

Each day he lives and is able to move around is a gift. A kidney transplant patient, he's been through not only the process of waiting for a donor, then the operation, but the endless side effects of the drugs that keep his body from rejecting the miracle that has kept him alive for five years as I write this. His spirit is inspiring. He's active in the community, does what he can around the house, and helps my sister at her dairy farm. Most importantly, he's always learning something new each and every day. He vicariously fishes through watching fishing shows and modifying the photos we email him via Photoshop. It's been two years since his visit. It might have been his last fish, and there will be no record of it. I held back. I didn't go fully into my experience with him. It's quite possibly more my loss than his.

The duck blinds were still a long way off, and the wading was anything but optimum. I decided to deposit my fish in the ice chest and met Scott at the boat. He delighted in my success. His face beamed with pride. Looking at his expression, I felt instantly grateful that I moved on from my past. I felt very blessed with his presence in my life.

I lifted the lid to the ice chest, and put my fish in my bag. There were three initialed plastic bags to keep our fish separate and clearly accountable. I sat on the edge of the boat and looked out over the water. While scanning the horizon, I thanked the fish for his sacrifice and prayed for his soul to be at peace.

"You look stunned," Scott said.

"It's hard for me to kill fish."

He nodded. It is for him, too.

Now, I hoped for a redfish for our client, who up until the day before had not caught a saltwater species on a fly. I also wished for Scott to bring in bigger fish.

I left the boat and headed toward the duck blinds. Scott said he'd join me in 15 minutes, the estimated time for me to reach the duck blinds on foot. The wading became even more difficult and I quickly grew weary. Ron was way ahead and on the spoil. I knew he was heading toward the flat along the Intracoastal. It was a good plan since the fish had all but disappeared in the lagoon. I turned around frequently, noticing that Scott continued to fish. I looked at my watch. I'd already been wading for 15 minutes, and I had a long way to go before I reached the shoreline. Thirty minutes later I reached the spoil, completely spent and thirsty. I was about out of water. My sandwich had long been burned off. I was anything but happy, especially when I noticed Scott was taking his time. I was growing impatient and psychically sent him a message that he'd better get moving, one that I felt he was ignoring. I started rehearsing my lecture. I obsessed that he was going to make us miss the weigh-in — another indication of how important this event really was to me. Unfortunately I didn't recognize this until much later. It would have saved me a lot of agitation. So would have another bottle of water and perhaps an energy bar.

I rounded the end of the spoil and heard the motor start up. He pulled up to the spoil as close as he could, and I shared my most recent thoughts, forgetting briefly at how blessed I was feeling just an hour or so before. He laughed. "I knew I had plenty of water to get up."

"Well I didn't." I sloshed through the water to the boat.

"You didn't need to." He took my rod and smiled.

He was right. I needed to trust his judgment. I needed to attend to my own business. He was the captain and knew his boat. He needed to go all the way into his experience, which he did, and landed an even bigger red. I was focused more on what he needed to do than what I needed to do...like possibly cross straight across the spoil to the ICW to try to catch more fish as Ron did.

With twenty minutes remaining before having to head to the dock, we gathered Ron and ran feverishly to Woody's Hole. This area along the west side of the ICW is just three miles from the mouth of the Arroyo. The flat at the entrance to this spot is known to have quite a few big trout in residence. Scott wanted a shot at a big trout (26 inches or better), Ron needed a redfish, and I vowed to go completely into my experience and fish for flounder. The twenty minutes passed quickly, and as I putted the boat back to Scott, I noticed Ron had a fish on his line. From a distance, it looked like another trout. Scott took over the helm and we joined Ron. He lifted a redfish out of the water and we all hooted and clapped. We brought the fish aboard and measured him. He looked big enough, but unfortunately came up an inch shy of being a keeper. Although we were a bit disappointed, we celebrated Ron's success. This was his third saltwater charter and he'd been fishless until our trip with him. Now he'd caught his first red on a fly. Most importantly he enjoyed his experience. At one point during the day, he turned to me and said, "Kathy, I now know I was born to be here, and to fish here."

I knew what he meant. Four years after first setting my eyes on this place, I still felt that I belonged here. The Laguna Madre makes my heart sing and she forever teaches me something new about myself. I'm like clay in her hands, and I'm being molded and shaped into a new art form, each rendition better than the one before, and only because I've surrendered to really being here and loving each precious moment I'm graced with — most of the time.

Back at the dock, time was of the essence. We had only a few moments to get fresh ice on our fish before making the 45-

minute drive to the weigh-in. Ron took off first to gather his kids, whom he left at the motel on the Island. He fished well despite the psychic distraction this must have been.

We arrived at the weigh-in ten minutes before the deadline. The crowd was thicker as many onlookers arrived to see the results of the bay division, and also the final weigh-in from the offshore division. We stopped for directions, and informed the lady who was directing traffic that we were there for weigh-in. She waved us on through to the closer parking area, and patted my arm. "Good luck." I smiled, appreciating the good wishes.

Scott and I walked as fast as we could to the line. Soon it was our turn, and I put my fish on the table. My name was called out and then the length and weight of my fish. I moved around to claim my receipt, and as I signed my name, I choked up, and fought back the tears. I was grateful for my sunglasses. I weighed in at just 5.38 pounds. To some this must have been silly, but they couldn't have known the magnitude of this feat. I'd not only entered a tournament, I'd seen it through the end. I'd weighed in my fish. My physical exhaustion was overshadowed by my elation.

We engaged in a brief visit with Skipper, whose luck, like Scott's, just wasn't there. Both had done really well in the past. The previous year Scott took first in the fly division. But by evening's end, we knew that wouldn't be the case. Our guest at the Inn weighed in two pounds more. The best we could hope for was just to place.

After a supper of soup and toast, I dropped into bed before 9:00 p.m., a rare luxury. Ten hours later, I rose, feeling happy and hopeful. Scott joined me after an hour, and we took our coffee to the porch. It was a calm morning and our thoughts turned to fishing. We reflected on what we could have done better. I wanted to go to the Mudhole, my magic spot, and didn't speak up. I should have. I needed to trust my wisdom as a fly fisher. Scott wanted to go back to the Trout Bar, but didn't. I even contemplated being left in the Mudhole/Trout Bar area with the kayak in the early part of the day, and going for broke, but I held my tongue. Perhaps if we'd both gone with our instincts, our results would have been better. All in all, we had a good time and enjoyed the experience. We approached it with our "heart's consent and made it a blessed event" — the Siddha Yoga theme for 2001. I didn't remember it often enough. It would have made my experiences more enjoyable if I did.

Morning passed quickly and it was time to travel to the Island for the awards ceremony. Scott came in third, and our guest Bob took second. The man to beat was from Brownsville, a member of our Laguna Madre Fly Fishing Association.

In actuality, I won, too. I broke through a lifelong pattern that had a death grip on me, one that I recognize not only in myself, but my parents and children as well. Even Scott has tinges of it in his psyche. There will be other tournaments. I may even win them in the public arena. And most likely, I'll have to face this sabotaging shadow again and again, but each time, I know I'll be stronger and it will be weaker.

Becoming the Elder, Remaining the Student

Late August 2001. Scott and I headed east on the Arroyo. As the sun rose, the sky turned pink and lavender. I slipped my arm through Scott's as he drove, and took a deep breath. It was so good to be back home again, to be on my home waters.

I'd gone to east Texas over the weekend to speak to the Texas Women Fly Fishers on fishing the Lower Laguna Madre. I'd taken my place as an elder in our ever-growing community of sister anglers. The thought still seemed a bit strange. *How did I come to such a place?* Speaking on fly fishing wasn't anything that I particularly aspired to do consciously, but when the call came, I could think of no better way of giving back than by accepting the invitation.

During the course of the weekend, I found myself in two alternating roles — both teacher and student. I received much needed casting evaluation and casting instruction from Bill Gammel, one of the top FFF instructors in the nation. I'd developed some bad habits during TIFT that were inhibiting my casting precision and creating some unwanted aches and pains in my lower left arm. A tweak here, a pause there, and soon I was back casting better than ever.

Then night came, and I was on. Speaking about my home waters came relatively easily. I knew her well, and it was also easy to share my path to success — that is casting and catching fish. I also allowed myself to show my less than perfect side and admit to the challenges I'd faced.

Denise Linn, author of *Sacred Legacies*, said "...our ancestors... didn't achieve everything all at once; they took small, indi-

Kathy wading the east side with a young angler.

vidual actions, which collectively made a contribution to the future. In our time on earth, we need only do our part and pass on the torch of our best efforts and our highest hopes to the next generation as they pass the torch to those who follow them."

This in essence was what I was doing, and what I had always done. It all started years ago when I was writing a relationships column and features on alternative health and women's issues. Now I was speaking and writing about fly fishing. The common thread weaving through this path is that I'm passionate about relationships and healthy living — and about fly fishing.

"When you live your life with care and a sense of connection to others, you will find that others will turn to you for help and your opinion. This is a sign that you are beginning to function as an elder in the circle of your family, school, church, or whatever you define as your community," said Linn.

Now my community was with fly fishers. I really started to wonder who was writing this script — especially after our trip to California. This was not what I imagined I would be doing when I "grew up." It was far better.

In February 2002, Scott and I spent ten days traveling and speaking to six different fly clubs in Southern California, from Santa Barbara to Los Angeles. It was a welcome break, and came when the fishing was particularly slow because of the frequency of blue northers, also referred to as cold fronts. We met so many incredible people, warm loving people who treated us like celebrities. I guess in some ways we were, but it was hard to fathom that we were becoming known for our fly fishing adventures. I was a little uncomfortable. After all, I was out of my element. I was usually the one hosting and nurturing, taking the supportive role. But after a time, I settled in and allowed myself to enjoy good company and the change of scenery.

During the last half of our stay we were hosted by George and Mary Chapman, notable elders in the fly fishing community. George is a masterful fly tyer, and we were lucky to have been gifted with several of his flies to display at the lodge. George and Mary are spirited octogenarians. They have the energy of whirling dervishes. He gardens and ties. Mary paints. Both are very talented artists in their own right.

One afternoon, while preparing for the evening's presentations, I was chatting with Mary in her kitchen. I mentioned that I never dreamed I'd be speaking about fly fishing, let alone doing it. She chuckled, and said, "Well when you let God take over, get ready for a ride."

I must admit while I didn't see it coming, I was enjoying the ride. And I was enjoying speaking about our home waters. After the first presentation, when we were back in our room, Scott said, "I've never seen you like this." He looked intrigued.

I was in the flow. The energy that comes over me when I'm teaching and speaking is similar to what wafts over me on the water or in meditation. When I'm deeply connected, I become a channel for God. The words or actions just happen, without premeditation. My little sense of self moves to the background and the bigger connected Self takes over. It's a very pleasant space to be in — no worries, no fretting, just being.

On that August morning, Scott was taking me once again for big trout. He'd found them tailing in good numbers over the weekend and wanted me to have my shot. As we stopped the boat near the Trout Bar, we immediately noticed streams of mullet passing by, and then the big black triangle — a tailing trout. Scott was out of the boat and ready. I was moments behind him. He sent me after the first one. By the time I was within range, it was upwind of me. I cast, and the line came back at me. Not so much because of the wind, but because I wasn't centered. I wasn't completely in the moment. I took a deep breath, and cast again. This time I put the trout down. I pushed my disappointment aside and continued to fish. Two hours passed. I'd had plenty of shots, several close encounters where Grandmother Trout taunted me with her knowing look — but still no fish.

Scott had wandered farther up the bar than I had, but still came back empty handed. However, it wasn't the fact that I didn't catch fish that bothered me, but that I didn't perform optimally, and therefore hadn't honored my teacher — him — and the knowledge and the opportunity that he had given me to be here in this very moment.

It was then that I realized how important it was for me to take my place as a teacher, and share whatever knowledge I've earned, but also to continue to gather knowledge via the mentors that cross my path. And that meant being accountable to whatever degree is deemed appropriate by that particular relationship.

In the case of my relationship with Scott, it meant that I needed to be fully equipped, and mentally and emotionally prepared to fish. I couldn't let my mind wander needlessly elsewhere. I took another deep breath, and prepared to do better at our next venue.

My teaching opportunities for my sister anglers are sporadic at best. At times there are lady anglers visiting Kingfisher whose talents far outshine mine. I bow to their wisdom and eagerly watch them cast, noting their form. I also respectfully request honest feedback regarding my techniques. I no longer cringe at my lack of experience. I'm wise enough and humble enough to know that I have a long way to go. The journey to mastery is never complete...it is a journey. But I also realize that I have learned a great deal and that I have a responsibility to share that with others who yearn to partake in the sport.

One weekend in late September we were visited by six fly fishers. Two were fellow TWFF members. Scott and I teamed up with Ann and Tibby, both of whom had little saltwater fly fishing experience. During the day, we switched off between the two, assisting them in their casting and sighting of fish.

About midafternoon, Tibby and I were near a spoil along the East Cut, an area near Port Mansfield, which is about 15 miles north from the mouth of the Arroyo. The water was crystal clear and the sun, after playing peek-a-boo all morning, was out and to our favor. Saltwater anglers groan at the thought of a cloudy day. You need the sun to sight cast to fish.

The ladies requested that Scott and I both fish, so I had my rod in hand and was using it for more than a pointer. Ann insisted that we were there to have a good time too and not just to keep our teaching eyes upon her. Besides, with her Alabamian charm, she admitted if she wanted to eat fish for dinner that night, she'd better have someone with a hot rod in hand.

Tibby's challenge was to see fish. So as we moved along together, I kept my eyes peeled not only for my opportunities but also hers. Suddenly, I saw a fish between us — upwind of me, but definitely within Tibby's range. I pointed to the fish. I crouched low to the water so as not to spook it as Tibby took her first cast. It was too far to the left of the fish. I encouraged her to reposition the fly closer. Once again she lifted the line and presented. This time the fish saw the fly and turned. Time stood still, and I know I for one, was unaware of anything else but Tibby, the fish, and my presence on the water. Suddenly, the strike.

My heart began beating faster as I yelled to her, "Rod tip up, Tibby."

She palmed the reel trying to contain his instinct to run.

"Let him run." I moved along side of her about ten feet away. "When he stops, then reel him in. He'll run several times before you land him."

The play continued, and a couple of runs later, Tibby landed a beautiful 19-inch redfish. I began to breathe again.

It was only then that I noticed Scott had walked up to us.

"That was so neat watching you two work together," he said. "Great job." He patted Tibby's shoulder as she cradled her fish.

Pictures came next. I took a couple of Tibby with her disposable camera. As she posed for the release shot, she said, "Do my thighs look thin?"

We laughed, and she lowered him to the water.

That fish made our day. I was probably about as excited about pulling an assist as I was at catching my own first red. There is nothing like that first red. Hers will forever be etched in my memory. Tibby has what it takes to go out there and achieve her angling goals. And I'm glad to have been able to take part in that experience with her.

Ann came up fishless by day's end, but she wasn't the least bit disappointed. She told Scott and me that she had no expectations. She only wanted to try something new and didn't need us to meddle into her angling form.

It has been hard not to place our expectations on those people who enter our lives, be they children or clients. We've learned that not everyone who crosses the Kingfisher Inn threshold will have the same capacity for invoking the huntress or hunter within, nor have the athletic ability needed to achieve mastery on this tough fishery. Not all anglers have the same passion for self-mastery. Some just want to fish. Others just want to catch fish. Our goal is to remain unattached to the outcome. We need only teach, guide, and host to the best of our ability, and allow the recipient to accept or reject our expe-

Tibby and Kathy, wading on a flat south of the East Cut spoils.

rience and hospitality to the level of their comfort. In some cases, that may mean some folks go home fishless and at times humbled. For others, the experience could outshine their highest expectations.

There is a saying from Eastern philosophy that states, "When the student is ready, the teacher will appear." I know from my own experience, when I'm ready to go to the next level of angling, or writing, or spiritual attainment, new mentors appear before me. Sometimes they're big trout or new adventures, and in some cases they take on human forms, teachers who stay with me for an hour, a day, or sometimes years.

Being a teacher means being willing to take your student to your level. It also means that you have a responsibility to keep on learning so you'll be able to keep the wheel turning. My friend Kris, a trainer and author, is a good example of this. He constantly pushes his body and his mind to new levels in order to keep ahead of his students. The more he learns the more he is able to share with others.

My dad is of the same ilk. He says you must learn something new each day. In 1997, he had a kidney transplant and has had a bevy of complications. But he goes on — helping my sister at her farm, serving on the school board, and now he and Mom are mentoring elementary school children. With such meaningful lives, it's hard to get them to come visit paradise once in awhile. They're elders in their own community.

When Magic Happens

December 29, 2001. The day dawned brightly and I knew nothing could keep me from the Bay. I hadn't been out on the water for personal fishing in more than a month. December heralded an unusual number of fishing clients, much to our delight. Added to this was the usual responsibilities that come with December — holiday shopping. I'm not a shopper, and I gave up many drop-dead gorgeous days to head to the mall for meaningful, conscious gifts for our children. While I accomplished this mission far beyond my expectations, I had passed up some pretty nice days, the days where our clients came back and said, "You should have seen the tails." But alas, while we live on the water, it is not always available to us, or us available to it, but on those days when it all comes together, it is magic.

Scott and I find that our passionate interests often compete with one another. We love fishing, we love writing, and we love to devote time to other facets of our spiritual practice — yoga, meditation and prayer, and reading. In the winter we have time for it all. Colder days, and fewer clients, and more time between those magical fishing days, make it possible. On this particular day, I rose at 5:00, and as I ventured into the kitchen, I was greeted by the mystical reflection of the moon dancing on the Arroyo. As I leisurely prepared breakfast for our guests, packed their lunches, and sipped my coffee, I stopped by the window frequently to savor this sight. Her image was nothing short of mesmerizing. Mother Mary was reminding me of her presence in my life once again.

Dharma Singh Khalsa, M.D., author of *Meditation as Medicine*, refers to this time of day as "amrit velt," time of nectar. He said, "This time, before the sun rises, is the stillest, sweetest time to be alive." I agree. The silence makes it possible to feel entirely alone and yet not, for it is at this time when all is quiet and not a word needs to be spoken that I can feel the Divine's presence without anything or anyone coming between us.

Our lifestyle changed dramatically when we moved to Arroyo City and opened our lodge. The demands on our time were difficult to adjust to, especially in the beginning. Besides preparing meals and spending hours on the water with guests, we were never sure when the door would open and someone would need our attention. In Virginia Beach, I had become accustomed to spending long hours alone while Scott maintained his private psychotherapy practice. Plus we had many hours of private time, and spent much of that in meditation and prayer. Neither did we share our personal space on a regular basis with anyone but our children and close friends, and even that was infrequent. Rarely did we have unexpected interruptions. As lodge owners, silence had become a precious commodity, and I savor every moment, especially in the early hours when it is sweetest.

By the time Henry, Jeff, and Scott joined me in the kitchen, the day was bright and sunny, with little wind — a saltwater fly fisher's dream. Breakfast was over in a hurry, and as I handed the guys their lunches, I said, "You know where the snacks are. I'm going fishing." A look of surprised interest crossed Jeff's face. As the door closed, I headed to the bedroom to prepare for a meditation. The action always starts a little later in the winter, so I had time to center myself before dressing for the flats.

Scott joined me, and we both entered the quiet. In an instant I felt deeply connected to Spirit. I'd worked many years to feel the spiritual energy descend upon me with such immediacy and intensity. These times were occurring with more frequency, although there were still those days when I struggled to set aside my troubling thoughts and "to do" lists. But after two decades of searching, I was at a point where there was little else that I wanted to do other than to feel that cloak of

Calm morning, sun breaking over the horizon on the LLM.

divinity around me at all times. However, I did not live a monastic life, and soon the world was calling me back.

I heard Scott stir and leave the room. Then the phone rang — an intelligence call from Skipper. The Holy Grail of Big Trout had been spotted to the south. Our hearts raced with excitement. IGFA record rang through my mind. Our recertified Boga Grip had arrived just the day before, for which I was grateful. While I wanted a record, I did not want to kill a fish to record it in the history books. The Boga Grip, a hand-held scale that also serves as a nifty tool to keep you from being wounded by "toothy critters" as our friend Wanda Taylor says, would allow us to have our cake and eat it too.

The phone rang again. This time it was a call for lodging. I stammered. I didn't want to stay behind to greet guests. Priorities are priorities. The woman must have felt my hesitation and promptly reminded me that she'd met me a couple months before. Problem solved. She knew the lay of the land and had toured the guesthouse. "I'm going fishing. I'll leave the key taped to the door. Make yourself at home. We'll be in this afternoon."

By 9:30 a.m., our boat was launched and we headed south. Without a GPS, a satellite-assisted navigational device, finding specific locations on the water could be a little tricky. Couple this with moving fish and it could be like searching for a needle in a haystack. We had to keep our eyes peeled for our intended prey. Soon we saw a dozen trout mingling together, then a small group of redfish; we stopped.

Scott was the first in the water; he headed northeast. After settling in Sam, our lab pup, with his toys, snacks, and water bowl, I headed slightly northwest, a hundred yards or so from Scott.

I took a deep breath, and tilted my face toward the sun, reveling in the warmth that sharply contrasted with the coolness seeping through my waders and several layers of undergarments. I repeated a mantra to regain my focus. Mantra repetition is a wonderful practice to keep the mind from wildly skipping from thought to thought. Chanting — repeating a mantra or a prayer in song-like form — is a ritual practiced in many religions. Mantras can be as simple as one word — "Om" or "Shalom" — or as lengthy as the *Hail Mary*, a Catholic prayer that is often repeated while saying the rosary. They help to bring the mind into one-pointed focus, and when the mind is quiet and at peace, God can step in and make some magic happen.

As Jesus said, "When thine eye is single, thy whole body is also full of light."

My sight was set on fish and only fish. However, I had yet to have the right amount of sunlight for optimum visibility. The sun's angle should be approximately 45 degrees to the east and west in order to be able to see under the surface of the water, and thus, see fish. This factor, along with a good pair of Polaroids, are necessary components of sight casting.

At this point, I couldn't distinguish a blob of grass from a fish. I continued to study the water. My patience and persis-

Scott holding Kathy's first sheepshead
(also the first time he's ever posed with one of her fish).

tence paid off. Soon I was able to see movement and the definable outline of a fish body. Color and markings were still unclear. At about the same time, Scott yelled over, "I'm beginning to see more now." The fish were moving from right to left, and he was the first in line. I kept my eyes peeled. Sheepshead were milling about in great numbers, mostly young ones. They often swam within a few feet of me before spooking.

Sheepshead are fun to catch on a fly rod. I caught my first a week or so before on a pink topwater popper — with a rattle — that Skipper tied. I had put it on just to give it a try and to be able to give him a report on how it did. Scott and I were on the east side in an area where the bottom is covered by turtle grass.

141

It was a calm morning and wakes could be seen for quite a distance. We saw lots of sheepshead tailing, and an occasional redfish cruising about. I cast the fly at an incoming wake, which formed a large V on the surface. I anticipated the strike from a mighty redfish, only to be completely flabbergasted as I saw the sheepshead's pearly whites come up to nab my fly.

These fish are rather short and plump, with black stripes on their bodies. They have big beautiful eyes, with several rows of teeth in their mouth, which liken them to their four-legged, landlocked namesakes.

I was so surprised at his presence that I missed the strike. Acting more like a bass than his usual timid self, the sheepshead came back for more, his mouth coming out of the water to nab the fly on the surface. I had him on the second strike. Catching a sheepshead on a topwater surprised many of my fellow anglers. They usually favor subsurface flies with reluctance even on the best of days. One client, however, came up with six hook-ups one day using a small spoon fly. Most spoon flies resemble a traditional gold or silver spoon used for spin rod. This gentleman molded his out of a plastic substance and reminded me of a fake fingernail, painted with glittery nail polish.

Today, however, the sheepshead were very wary, but it didn't concern me. I had my sights set on Grandmother Trout. I concentrated on a half circle of water, scanning an area from 30 to 70 feet around me. She appeared. A large trout, not huge, but large; a record by any means. I cast once, but did not compensate for the wind and it landed too far to the left and out of her line of sight. My heart skipped a beat. She didn't spook. I cast again, and this time the fly landed beyond her by about a foot. I started to curse my inaccuracy but stopped when I saw her turn and follow my red and black Lefty's Deceiver. Then the take. My heart leapt with excitement. I stripped the line once to set the hook and raised my rod. She swam toward me without reservation. I reached back as far as I could and began stripping feverishly to take up the slack. With her fast approach, I knew I could never turn the reel quickly enough to start playing her off of it. My only hope was to keep stripping — and fast. It wasn't enough. I stretched my casting arm up as far as it would go to take up even another inch or two. The line went limp. She played me like a pro, and instead of fleeing in the face of danger, she faced me head on and challenged me. I could only bow to her wisdom.

Scott yelled over to me. "You had too much slack."

"She ran right at me."

He shook his head. "Nothing you could do about that."

I agreed and was far from disappointed. I'd taken a gigantic leap to landing my big trout. I had a hook-up, and the day was still young.

I looked back at Sam. He had his head up, apparently interested in the action. When he saw me look at him, he laid back down. He wasn't eager to get in the water. A water dog he is, a fool he is not. He likes it warm. Assured that he wasn't eating the console or the rod holders on the boat, I resumed my fishing. I watched Scott walking stealthily along. "You can really see them now," he yelled.

I nodded and took a few more steps before stopping and observing my surroundings. Far to the northeast a layer of fog was drifting toward us. Except for the beached drum boats, where trotline fishers once stored their gear, there wasn't another boat in sight. We were alone in this magical paradise, with only the din of boats running the channel to remind us that we were far from having this place all to ourselves.

I lowered my eyes and readjusted my vision to the water. My eyes immediately fell to a fish not 20 feet from me. We eyed each other, both of us unmoving. It was a trout. And then I saw another fish, and another, which I identified as redfish, and then another trout, all moving except for the first. I turned my head slowly, to convince her that I wasn't interested in her presence, but on the lookout for other fish. To my astonishment the water around me was vibrating. A full semicircle from right to left was filled with a herd of fish. I spotted another trout. I could not move my rod. I could barely breathe. I wasn't even sure if my heart was beating. For a brief second I considered what they might do to me. After realizing the silliness of this thought, I rose to the opportunity to catch a fish, a big fish. Be it redfish or trout, the mother lode was at my feet. I cast once into the crowd and I saw the flurry of bodies readjust themselves after my sloppy intrusion. Thankfully perfect presentation wasn't called for in this situation, and on my second cast, I had an immediate take. "Wahoo." I yelled, delighting in the hook-up.

"What is it?" Scott asked.

"I believe it's a red." I continued to play the fish. He ran hard, determined to be free of my grasp. His friends remained nearby, seemingly unruffled by my presence. "Scott, you've gotta get over here. They're still all around me. C'mon. Take some of this action."

He stayed behind. "Pay attention to your fish," he called.

I had been so enthralled by the sheer number of fish that milled around me that I had forgotten that I had to do more than hold my rod. I put my consciousness back to the fish. He had honored me with taking my fly, now I had to honor him with my complete presence. He fought nicely, making several runs. Soon it was just the two of us doing our dance, alternately bowing to each other's authority. His friends had scattered and Scott observed from a distance.

I could feel him drumming through my rod. I spoke to him. "Don't worry sweety, you're not dinner." He came closer and I could see he was a big beauty.

Scott made his way over to me as I was about to lift him out of the water. "Fred would call him a pig," he said.

I grinned from ear to ear. This was clearly the biggest fish I had ever landed.

"We got to put him on a stringer and get a picture," Scott said.

The camera was back at the boat. I hesitated, but agreed. There are varying degrees to the practice of ahimsa — the act of doing no harm, which Gandhi espoused as one of the greatest virtues. Today, it was strictly catch and release. However, I told this one he was going to be a star and we needed a photo. I marveled at the shimmering blue outlining his tail as Scott put him on the stringer. "You need to concentrate on your big trout," he said as he walked away with the fish.

Kathy with December Red

I didn't argue. Fish on a stringer are like pesky puppies and tend to get underfoot at the most inopportune times — like when you're about to cast to an even bigger prize.

It wasn't long before I began seeing the fish appear around me again. This time they were in twos and threes. A group of three was coming toward me from the northwest. I could see the outline of their bodies on the edge of the pothole. The wind was light, but out of the north as well. The visibility was good, the casting doable even into the wind, as long as I punched out the line with intention. Half-hearted attempts are time — and energy — wasters. In this case, each time, I let my attention lapse a bit, my line collapsed not far from the tip of my rod. The cast to this group of redfish had to be 50 feet and perfect, meaning right on top of their heads. Redfish do not like to be ambushed by a fly landing ahead of them and crossing their paths. Most often they strike out of instinct rather than hunger. The element of surprise must be enlisted to achieve success.

The moon was just a day away from being full. This not only interrupts my sleeping patterns but the fish's as well. They feed under the light of the moon, making them finicky in the light of day. I planted the fly right in the midst of them. Competition makes them more aggressive. I had a take. The others scattered. As I played the fish, the thought crossed my mind that I had already had one hook-up, one landed fish, and I was on with another. Scott hadn't had much more than a couple of follows by that time. I chased any co-dependent thoughts from my mind that might have sabotaged my efforts and went back to my fish. He was another big red and had circled me once before showing any signs of admitting defeat.

I heard Scott yell. He was hooked up. "We got a double."

"All right!"

He reeled in a nice red, about 23 inches in length.

I landed my red and struggled with the fly. While I had caught him in the lip, the fly just did not want to come out. My forceps, which I rarely use, were on the boat. I had stuffed my stringer and my fly box in my jacket pockets so not to be encumbered in the deeper water with my pack and my Strip 'n Aid.

"I can't get the fly out." I hated to ask for help. Having done it once before on a similar day a year before when I was up by two fish, I cringed waiting for Scott's impatient response. There wasn't any. I guess we'd grown in a year. I wasn't whining this time. I had weighed all my options, including cutting the fly off. But I couldn't send that fish off with a fly in its mouth. I truly was in a fix, not a damsel in distress.

I made my way toward Scott holding the fish close by. We weren't that far apart, but I knew he was thinking we were wasting valuable sunlight and fishing time. I held my fish up for him. He was bigger than the one on the stringer, but I didn't want to put him in temporary shackles as well. Scott struggled with the fly, but finally it let lose. I thanked him for his cooperation and sent him on his way.

I resumed fishing, but noticed that I was particularly antsy and unfocused. I was feeling anxious. I continued my efforts, but was either not seeing fish or making deplorable presentations. I took a moment to focus inward and discovered that my bodily functions were demanding attention.

Redfish in the water

Scott about to release his trout

I wish I could remember to do this off the water more often. When I do take the time to check in with myself, I'm able to ward off any further build-up of stress, usually by taking a little time for myself, or attending to something that I've been avoiding, like much of the paperwork it takes to run a business.

I tried to buy some time, but alas it was in vain. The fish seemed to have disappeared or were uninterested in any well-put fly. I headed back to the boat. But not before witnessing Scott's second catch — a 24-inch trout.

"You caught my fish again." I chuckled. There was a time when I would have meant it, but I've come to believe that you always catch your share, as a client of ours once stated. It just wasn't my time for trout.

Scott held up his fish. She was a beauty. He put her on the stringer for more photos. We seem never to have enough, and with the water temperature cooler, there was little danger of her dying while we continued our fishing. Trout are fragile creatures, and in the warmer weather when the oxygen levels in the water are lower, they tire quickly and soon succumb to the excessive stress of being caught — and even released.

Our friend Bud Rowland, released a 10-pound trout that would have been a new IGFA world record — only to find her belly-up the next day. Not only did a record go unattained, but her spirit wasn't honored as food for the table either.

Back at the boat I tended to my own needs and gave Sam a treat. Scott too was heading back. We'd been away from the boat for three hours. It felt like a few minutes. As I stared out at the water, I questioned whether or not the fishery had indeed shut down, or if it was merely that my attention was drawn elsewhere, and, therefore, I was not as aware of the opportunities before me, or perhaps not in the proper state of mind to take advantage of shots I had. That question remained with me.

We returned home at 5:00, surprised that the day had gone by so quickly. Henry and Jeff were behind us as we entered the Arroyo. They pulled into the Inn moments after we had arrived home as well. Scott and Elvia, other guests who also fished on their own that day, had arrived at port ahead of all of us.

Scott tended to the boat, while I headed to the kitchen. As quickly as I could, I put out snacks and started warming the chili that I had the foresight to make the day before. Jeff walked in. He looked dejected.

"How'd you do?" I asked.

"Not good. One little red. I threw everything at them, and they just wouldn't take my fly." He dropped his jacket on the back of a chair and headed back out the door to gather more of his gear from the boat. He turned. "How did you do?"

"One hook-up on a big trout, and two 27-inch reds. Used a red and black deceiver."

"I threw that at them, too." He shook his head and walked out of the door — speechless. I went back to the kitchen, pondering the situation.

Henry came in and went to the fridge for a beer. Henry and Jeff are part of what used to be called "The Scooter Society", until Henry defected and bought an HPX Mirage, a flats boat manufactured by Maverick. Henry and his fishing compadres have become more like brothers than guests and readily make themselves right at home. "I heard you got into fish," he said.

I nodded and retold my story about my hook-up and my two reds, and also about being surrounded by the hundred or so fish. He looked shocked.

From the living room, Jeff said, "Henry, I'm going to leave you home tomorrow and take Kathy out on the boat with me."

We all chuckled. They retreated to their room, and I headed to the guest house to invite our other guests to share chili with us. I found Elvia in her toasty warm room reading a book. Her Scott came in and said, "I heard you had two 27 inchers." I nodded. He shook his head. "I didn't see a thing."

With as much humble finesse as I could muster, I muttered a few words and dashed back to the house so I could bathe before dinner. My success was briefly discussed over dinner, very briefly. It seemed to be a subject that created a bit of discomfort with my fellow anglers. I silently pondered the deeper meaning of my success, which I later reviewed with Scott. The fly fishers at the table were all much more experienced than I. All had fished in other parts of the world for bonefish, permit, tarpon, reds, and with varying degrees of success. I had fished here, in the Laguna Madre, exclusively for the last four years. By conventional terms, my success in sheer numbers had been meager at best. But today, I had out fished all of them, including my husband. How could that be?

I expect I was in the flow. I allowed life to lead me, instead of the other way around. My meditation was truly the starting point for such a magical day — that and being open to the beauty of nature's surroundings. Had I not been aware of the mystical appearance of the moon dancing on the Arroyo, I might not have been conscious enough to be present for the fish. When we curtail our busyness and allow ourselves to enjoy the wonders of nature, it paves the way for that mystical connection with all of creation. It allows us to feel and be totally present in the moment, and not distracted by our fears, worries, and the concerns of our daily lives.

There have been at least 54 full moons since I've lived here, most of which probably danced on the Arroyo as today's had. None stopped me in my tracks like this particular one. She caught my breath and I was drawn back to view her image until it was no longer visible — but only because I made myself available to her. I allowed her into my consciousness and awareness, blocking out any distracting thoughts which might have spoiled the magic of the moment.

I also surrendered any agenda I might have had and tamed my eagerness to be out on the water to make time for God. I was fully present and willing to be in communion with the divine power that oversees all of our comings and goings — including the fish. Perhaps the fish were aware of my alignment with our Creator, and felt comfortable coming forth so readily.

That was likely the only factor that helped me to rise above the compendium of experience held by my fellow anglers, Scott included. Having suffered from a bad cold for over two weeks, he still wasn't physically comfortable to sit for meditation for any period of time; and, therefore didn't feel as connected to the Divine as he yearned to be.

We all have our own ways to unwind and shake off the psychic burden of the stresses of our life. For some this means fishing, but I've heard many anglers admit it takes some time to settle in. My approach is to attune myself with some other form of practice — yoga or meditation — before I fish, even if only for a few moments. This usually shortens the amount of time I need to adjust to the feel of my rod, to get my wading legs, and to see fish.

Unfortunately, I didn't feel that it was my place to share my musings with my fellow anglers.

Ten days later, my hypothesis was confirmed. It was a beautiful January day; the kind that Scott and I long for. Winds of 10 mph or less to start with, bright sunshine, and temperatures in the low 70s. Winter fishing on the Lower Laguna is one of the best-kept secrets. With the tides of winter dropping very low, the fish seem to congregate in greater numbers in less space, making our chances of scoring even higher.

On this day, the tides were low and the fish were present. I was not. My body was, but my mind and spirit lagged far behind, despite my best efforts to bring myself into alignment. I was eager to fish, to be out in nature. The last week had been trying at best, and my day started without a good meditation. Inwardly I struggled with the heaviness of great sorrow. Outwardly, our son's dog Oakie was visiting, and he had taken up the habit of flying over the fence with an effortless bound. I couldn't relax as he and Sam romped around the backyard — and sometimes beyond. I touched Spirit briefly in my quiet time, and then threw in the towel. I roused myself from my lotus position, and dressed for fishing.

The phone rang. New clients. I had to scramble to make their expectations fit within our upcoming trip to California. I called Skipper and Judi for back-up. In the background I heard Scott answer another call and say, "She's on the phone with a client."

I pasted the key on the door for our Winter Texans who I thought might be arriving that day. Scott hitched the boat to the Rodeo. I put on my waders, collected the dogs — Oakie in the kennel, Sam on the bed. I hid Baba, our new kitty, in the bathroom with his food and his litter. The only thing he had in common with Sam and Oakie was his color. He deplored the sight of them, and even though he'd only been a member of the family for little more than a week, he had taken a liking to Scott and me in a big way and displayed his jealousy toward Sam and Oakie by baring his long white fangs. I joined Scott in the car. I put my seat belt on as Scott eased out of the driveway. Then he stopped abruptly.

"Shana called."

I contemplated using the cell phone from the boat launch, but we both decided against it. Calling her was important. It had been less than a week since we learned the news of losing a dear friend, the mom to Shana's best buddy Laura, and the woman who was my dearest friend for such a long, long time. We raised our babies together, tie-dyed baby clothes, took our kids hiking so they could make fairy houses and play with their imaginary friends. We shopped and talked and were there for each other during very difficult times. Now Karen was gone, and yet somehow I knew she wasn't. I'd felt her presence in the last week more closely than I had in the last dozen years when geography and life circumstances took me far from the base from which our friendship was formed.

Shana was going to the memorial service in New York to be with Laura. I was not. In my moments of silence and contemplation, I felt Karen implore me to be there for her girls when they needed me most, after the dust had settled and the sadness crept into their lives at unexpected moments. I knew in my heart it was what she wanted, not for me to take days away from my home and my husband and our business to make a cameo appearance in a place I hadn't been for so many years.

Shana's tears were readily apparent. "I'm not doing so well."

"I'm having a sad day, too." Spiritually we all knew Karen was in a better place. But we still had our sadness. We had our loss, which we were all dealing with in our own private ways. To top it off, Shana was also angry with me.

"I was really mad when you decided not to go, because I felt like I needed you there."

For the past few days I suspected her lack of contact with me was about just that. "I know..."

"Don't defend yourself. Please just listen." She choked a sob.

A wave of relief washed over me. I didn't have to defend myself — something I never felt comfortable *not* doing in times past. I had a habit of having to justify my position. But because I was honoring my decision, Shana was too, despite having to travel to New York in the coming days alone for a very difficult task.

"I'm just tired of being the strong one all the time. I can't even find anyone to take me to the airport. They're all too tired or in a bad mood. I'm always the one that has my shit together. I'm always the one to be there for everyone else."

I listened until she finished. Then we laughed together when I reminded her that she seemed to attract some unreliable friends of late.

We come from a long line of strong women. My memory rests on my own mother. She was raised by a grandmother and mentored by loving women neighbors, having in one sense lost her own mother to mental illness. She's had a tough life, fraught with many emotional blows. As a result, she has raised two tough daughters. I have a pistol-packing sister who makes her living in dairy farming. She's physically tough and has the wherewithal to put herself through long, hard days, much harder than I could ever agree to. I think I've seen Mom cry once. I cry though, a lot. I just let it rip, unable to stuff it in, the way my mom seems to do. In turn I've raised a tough daughter, who is probably more like my mother in some ways than me. She doesn't cry as often, but she does let her feelings be known. For us, being strong women is both a blessing and a curse. As I'm reminded time and time again, the Lord never gives us more than we can handle. Shana and I have had tough times to face, and many challenges lain before us. But somehow we've weathered them, and grown from it. We've gotten closer.

Psalms 29:11 states, "The Lord will give strength unto his people; the Lord will bless his people with peace."

With the air cleared, peace once again resided between us. Shana moved on with her day — and me as well. I felt relieved that we were able to speak of our feelings, and that she felt safe to express hers to me. It makes for a special closeness that is often hard to describe. Something I have only recently come to know with my own mother.

Scott's patience was to be rewarded. I joined him in the car and filled him in on my conversation with Shana. We launched the boat, and I took a deep breath. Time to fish.

Skipper once again came through with the hot tip of the day, and we headed southeast of Duncan's Channel. We became momentarily diverted by a large group of redfish congregating just south of Bird Island on the west side of the channel. But we'd blown them up as we boated through and decided to continue onward.

As we planed along the flats, I watched for fish, but my mind reviewed my conversation with Shana, and my decision. I'm never one to make a decision without weighing all the options, and my heart usually wins out. Today my mind was vying for superiority. I was now justifying my decision to myself, making mental lists of all the reasons why I didn't have to travel to New York, which included my mother being there for Shana.

We found fish. We got out and began our wade. My troubled thoughts continued to overshadow my quest for fish. I chanted the mantra, "Om Navah Shivaya," — "I bow to the Lord who resides within me" — over and over and over. It helped me stay out of my sadness and the horror of imagining Karen's last moments. My imagination can be a great asset as a writer, but at other times it becomes my greatest enemy. I needed to stay with the Truth and with my heart.

I saw a fish and cast. I overshot and lined him. It spooked and dashed off taking several of his friends with him. Scott yelled, indicating that he'd hooked up. I turned back toward the water in front of me; a tail appeared. Then another. I got into position and cast, but it was too short. The tails went down. I searched the water for where they might have gone. I saw them far to my right. My line collapsed like a wet noodle. I cursed. Scott hooked up again. The scenario repeated until he was five up on me and I'd lined as many fish as I've caught in the last few trips. All the while I struggled to control my mind and be totally present to fish, to live my life.

I practiced my casting, focusing my attention and intention on a spot in the water. I hit it time and time again. My mind wandered and I cast again. The line fell far to the left. I refocused and shot the line. I hit my target. I knew this mind-body stuff worked, and yet I couldn't always turn it on and keep it on. It was frustrating. Just a few days earlier, my friend Mary reminded me that I have high expectations for myself and often pursue perfection to a fault. Today was no different, I felt I should be able to be present, I should be able to catch fish, and I should be able to see the grand design in Karen's death. I shouldn't be afraid of my own.

But I was. No matter how many times, I've caught glimpses of "heaven," in my meditation, no matter how many times I've felt my ego-self slip away and I've merged completely with God, I can't sustain it. I've not yet reached enlightenment no matter how much I've practiced.

The former spiritual head of Siddha Yoga, Baba Muktananda said, "It is only because of the ego that we have to do sadhana, or spiritual practice. We do not have to attain God, because we are already God...Yet we cannot know that all-pervasive great Being while bound to our separateness."

I still have a hard time always believing and feeling God within me. Spirit is still a force outside of me much of the time. This feeling invokes in me a sense of eventual abandonment, and I fear facing an eternal loneliness.

I know the only way to rid myself of this fear is to put my improper ego in check, and in doing so I will achieve heaven on earth. As Jesus said, "By losing yourself you shall find yourself; by dying you shall live." I don't believe he was speaking only of the literal sense of dying. I believe he was speaking of our ego.

In part, I was also afraid I hadn't really lived, and that was a source of much grief for me. I'd let a lot of fear, worry, and living according to the values and expectations of others waste many years of my life. It saddened me greatly. Karen's death was a wake-up call, a reminder that we are not immortal, and that we have only a certain amount of time to achieve what we've come to this planet to accomplish. I truly believe that we are all called to perform a certain role, to be of service in some special way. I knew, without having to have my own near-death experience, that I had not honored my soul's commitment to my life mission. I also knew that it was time to take steps to do just that. My decision not to travel to New York was just one step.

Scott headed back to the boat, and putted toward me. I had one more shot and blew it big time. I climbed on board. "I figured it was time to move," Scott said. "I was afraid if I caught one more fish you might not sleep with me again."

His comment brought a grin to my face. "I was getting ready

to come back and just sit. I'm really snakebit today." I refrained from telling him why. I knew my enemy and I was trying valiantly to win the battle.

We boated to the east and saw no fish in the shallower water, although it was pretty. I wished they were there. The skinnier water and the sandy bottom seemed less harsh and more welcoming. I felt like perhaps I'd have a better chance there. We returned to the transition area where the water is a bit deeper and where the fish were. The transition area has a mottled bottom—part grass, part sand, with a yellowish cast to the water. We stopped several hundred yards north of where Scott picked me up.

He left the boat. Turning back he said, "Now catch fish."

I nodded, taking one last bite of my energy bar and a swig of my sports drink. Clients get full course meals on board. However, when personally fishing, Scott and I sustain ourselves, even for full days of fishing, with water, juice, sports drinks, and bars in all shapes and flavors. Our priority is to fish. We can eat on land, and usually do voraciously after a long day on the water.

I climbed out of the boat and watched for fish. Scott hooked up. I stared at him in disbelief. Fish were once again all around me. Then one red came so close that it spooked me when I saw it. The light was getting lower, and the fish were becoming harder to see. Scott landed his seventh fish, and headed back to the boat, practicing his casting into the wind as he went. I contemplated joining him in his practice, seeing the futility in my catching a fish this day. But then I figured I wouldn't do much better with casting practice. I turned around and concentrated on finding a fish.

Suddenly, I felt very alone, and very sad. I saw fish coming. I cast into the group and hooked up. "This one's for you, Karen." It broke off. The tears followed. I cried long and hard, wiping my tears from my face with my cold hands. I cried for the friend I lost and for the times we once shared. In the past week I'd remembered so many of our moments, moments that were buried in the depths of my mind. A purple Gap sweatshirt. I was with Karen when I bought it. I no longer have it and I no longer have her friendship the way it once was, and haven't for some time. It was more than her death that caused this grief. My path took a hard right and I'm here fly fishing in South Texas. She was my New York moment. We shopped, we cooked, and we hiked. We shared the simple pleasures of life. Some painful ones, too. Her friendship made the intolerable events of my past tolerable. I sobbed aloud, grateful that Scott couldn't hear me and that no one else was around. I became suddenly in touch with all of my loss. Lost dreams, failed relationships, and the distancing from loved ones. Some would call it necessary. At that moment it seemed a bit much. But as the Mother Lagoon embraced me, with waves lapping at my knees, and the wind drying my tears, I was beginning to see the wisdom in all of it. I knew that one day with the help of the Divine Mother, I would accept it completely as well.

I, too, am tired of being strong. Yet I realized that I've had no choice but to be. It's the path I have chosen, and I must accept all of it — the joy and the sorrow. It's all a part of life and there is no escaping it. There will be days when I fish well, and there will be days when I don't. There can be no light without darkness, no joy without sorrow. It's balance, the yin and the yang.

The tears ceased and I was once again filled with a sense of peace.

Scott floated toward me on the boat. He hooked up again.

"All right, I may not sleep with you again." I laughed as I climbed aboard. "Only kidding." I looked away so he couldn't see my red, blotchy face.

"I broke off. I didn't want to take any chances," he said.

We chuckled.

The day was about a lot more than catching fish — or not catching them. I returned home, with my husband, my friend by my side. As we entered the Arroyo, I shared the musings of my day with Scott — a confession of sorts. I felt lighter and happier. Even as Shana came to recognize the authenticity in my decision and the way it allowed her trip to unfold according to God's plan, I was beginning to see how perfectly the Plan was working in my life. With Scott I've shared a lot of joy.

We share the simple things. Sunsets and sunrises; herons dancing on the dock; the smiles on our clients faces when they catch
their first red. He's patient with my process — whether it's
learning to cast a fly rod, mothering my children in a better
way, or grieving over losses out of my control. His presence in
my life is proof that the light truly does appear at the end of
the tunnel.

On to Sea School

March 2002. The subject of my captain's license had been background noise in our consciousness since we began our operation. It seemed to be always looming far off in the distance, something we occasionally acknowledged as a good idea, but someday.

Someday came sooner than we expected — and in its usual head-spinning whirlwind.

The signs were becoming readily apparent that we were growing faster than we ever expected. In many cases, when four or more anglers were gathered, it meant that we often had difficulty finding other guides who were free to work with us. Still, in my mind, sea school was at least a good season away.

Three weeks after our trip to California we were on the road again. Neither Scott nor I were looking forward to being away from home for another week. We'd barely gotten back into our routine of meditation, exercise, writing, and eating in our simple, healthy way. But we were asked to speak at the Shallow Water Expo in Houston, and we had a booth. We had to go.

From past experience, we knew that something good would come out of this trip, despite our misgivings about leaving our oasis on the Arroyo. So we went, and more good came of it than we dreamed.

Our talks were a hit, which didn't go unnoticed by the show's producer. People were not only interested in fishing the Lower Laguna, my presence alongside of Scott as an equal was a unique draw. It made us accessible to fly fishers of all levels of experience — young and old, male and female. People who attended our talks came by our booth and became even more enticed to pay us a visit. Within a week of coming home, we had several bookings from that show alone.

Our personal appearances, which we'd done very few of up to this point, along with Scott's articles in the major fly fishing magazines, were drawing the attention of fly fishers from around the country. At times we looked back and realized our business grew almost overnight; at others, we were just barely beginning to breathe a sigh of relief. It had taken a lot of hard work and prayer for us to reach the point where we were making our operation known. We were becoming part of the fly fishing community, and it felt great.

During the show, we had the chance to see and meet several guides and other authorities in the business whom we'd heard of, and visa versa. Captain Sally Moffett of Rockport was one of them.

The women's fly fishing circle is a relatively small one in Texas, particularly in saltwater. There are a few "names" out there, and hers was one that I've heard mentioned many times. During a slow moment, I wandered down to her booth. She was sitting in Chuck Scates booth, another well-known Texas fly fishing guide, who operates out of the Redfish Lodge also in Rockport. Scott and I had met him a year before at a Laguna Madre Fly Fishing Association outing on South Padre Island. I nodded to him, since we had a chance to visit earlier, and walked up to Sally. Extending my hand, I said, "Sally, I'm Kathy Sparrow." She was on her feet, with a big grin across her face.

Chuck said, "I had no idea you two hadn't met. I would have introduced you earlier," referring to my earlier visit to his booth.

"I've heard of Sally many times, but we haven't met." Truth was I heard that she too was after ladies' IGFA trout record(s), a category that had been created only in the last couple of years. While I had cringed at hearing that months before, upon meeting her I immediately thought, *Heck, let's work together.*

We took a few steps into her booth, and our conversation was off. I felt like I had found a long lost friend. We covered a lot of ground in a few minutes. I was aware of several men waiting to gain her attention. She seemed unhurried. And then she said, "You need to get your captain's license."

I nodded. "I know. We're talking about next winter." I paused. "I heard it's tough."

"You can do it." She gave me the name of the school she attended. "It'll be great. Women's fly fishing is really taking off, especially saltwater. You need to be in on it."

This time I smiled. Her words rang true. I was only partially involved. I tagged along on the boat as a teacher, unable to operate it legally without my license. My captain's license would allow me to go fully into my experience. Not having it kept me slightly removed. In a sense I hadn't made a full commitment to our business. I was afraid I wasn't good enough. I was hedging.

I went back to my booth, tucking the information into my pocket.

Upon our arrival back at home, Scott and I delved into the pile of mail and unending household chores. In particular my stepson was due to arrive on Saturday, and we needed to get his room ready. He arrived without a glitch. One of his first remarks was, "I've got an extra week of vacation. My spring break isn't until after Easter."

Scott and I exchanged horrified glances. Ryan is time challenged. He has no concept of days, weeks, months, or even hours. They are all about the same to him. On one hand, he is definitely living in the present moment. On the other it's scary. We pray that he'll grow out of it. For days, he insisted that all his friends were in school. Scott called Ryan's stepdad. It was true. He and Ryan's mom assumed spring break was the way it always had been — the week before Easter. When they checked the school's website the night before his departure and discovered it was the week after instead, it was too late to make a change in plans. Ryan came for his visit, missing three and half days of school. Little did we know divine timing was in action once again.

When we weren't visiting family, I used the week to clean, write, and even caught up on a few phone calls. One particular morning I was deep in conversation with my friend Jane, when I saw Scott enter the room with the cordless phone in his hand. I heard him say, "It starts Monday. I'll tell her."

I stopped in my tracks. "Jane, hold on....What?" I looked at Scott.

"Sea school starts Monday on the Island." My heart raced and my palms became sweaty. My stomach flip-flopped. I tried to go back to my talk with Jane, but my mind was whirling. I got off the phone.

Scott filled me in on the details and encouraged me to call Captain Pat Kelley and find out more for myself. Ryan wandered around the kitchen all ears, wondering what was going

Kathy and Ryan boating along the ICW

163

on. I wondered myself. Suddenly I felt like I was a remote con-
trolled human being, gently being steered in a particular direction. I tried to find the brake and couldn't. I picked up the
phone. Captain Kelley answered. I listened more to the tone of
his voice than his actual words. He informed me we'd be in
class for two weeks, from 6 to 10 every evening and all day
Saturday.

"I need to sleep on this. I'll call you tomorrow," I said. For
the rest of the day I wandered around in a semi-altered state.
It was beginning to feel like one of those situations that I just
couldn't say no to — exciting on one hand, frightening on the
other. I was being stretched out of my comfort zone. I wanted
to cry out, *Haven't I grown enough?*

The next morning Scott and I took Ryan fishing. I manned
the boat. It was an interesting experience to drive our new
boat for the first time from dock to dock, with a less than confident 13-year-old and our year-old lab. I did well. No one was
tossed overboard, even on my take-offs in shallow water. My
confidence rose. I returned home and called Captain Kelley.

"I'll come by tomorrow to pick up your tuition," he said.
Now I really knew this was meant to be. I didn't even have to
travel the 50 minutes to his office to make my payment.

Monday arrived — the first day of sea school, and April
Fool's Day. Deep inside I knew I wasn't a fool. I knew this was
something I had to do. Scott had a client out on the water, and
I spent the day tying up loose ends. The next two weeks would
place great demands on me. At 3:30 the phone rang. Scott said,
"When do I have to be back?"

I felt myself become annoyed. "I need to leave here at 4:45."
He had the car at the launch. I envisioned having to change
my clothes and bike three miles to fetch the car, and then take
another shower. I felt squeezed.

"I'll be there by 4:30."

At 4:45 I was pacing. He wasn't back. I had to leave. He
arrived at 4:50. I was off, after giving him a brief kiss, and
telling him there was soup in the pantry. This was different! I
usually dote on him, making nearly every meal. It's not expected. I like doing it. But here I was telling him to fend for

himself while I went out to explore new vistas — and I felt good about it.

I arrived 20 minutes before class started, which was highly unusual for me. With so many variables, such as phones and unexpected visitors at the lodge, I'm usually running late. I realized when I took my seat, I let nothing prevent me from leaving on time. I even built in a cushion just in case something unexpected did come up.

A pile of books laid before me. The excitement rose once again, and continued like waves. Two other classmates joined me. One was a fellow fly fisher, the other a shrimper. We settled into the administrative details of the class, which took most of the evening. Pat called an early night, sending us home with a reading assignment. I was home by 9:00, eager to share the events of the evening with Scott. My enthusiasm for the intellectual challenge was spilling over. There was also some apprehension.

In a session just a month or so before with Darla where we discussed sea school, she mentioned it that it felt to her like a formality. All the signs were pointing to this development in my fly fishing career. However, that evening it felt like more of a major challenge than a mere formality. Four tests loomed before me, the toughest, or so I was told was just three days away. I had to learn "the rules of the road," and make a 90 or better to pass. It was a 30 question, closed book test, on light configurations, sounds, signals, buoys, channel markers, and distress signals. I looked ahead at my schedule. I had a hair appointment on the books on the day of the test. I checked my roots. They'd have to wait. I called and canceled my appointment. Now I knew I was serious.

For the next three days, I studied every chance I got. It was my priority. I had a routine. Rising at 5:15, I prepared breakfast for our guests. By 7:00 they were on the dock, with lunches in hand. By 8:00 the kitchen was clean and the floors had been swept. I did 20 minutes of yoga and ate some semblance of breakfast, usually a protein shake and a half a bagel. Then I studied for a couple of hours, took a break, and studied some more. I usually studied for four to six hours a day, knowing I had to finish and be dressed by 3:30. Then I switched gears and began preparing dinner, along with a detailed list for Scott on how to finish the preparations so he could serve our guests. Then by 5:00 I was on my way to school.

Wednesday night arrived. I was thoroughly enjoying the learning process and the intellectual challenge it presented me. I couldn't remember when I'd been more excited about learning, except for when I took Russian ten years or so before. Pat introduced more material. There was so much to remember, and I was afraid I wasn't ready. The night passed quickly. I called Scott on my way home. "Don't wait up for me. I'm going to study before I come to bed." The dark hand of fear clenched my throat.

The house was silent when I arrived home. Not even Sam came out to greet me. I walked into the kitchen. My stomach growled. Sleeping and eating were now luxuries. I could feel the pounds dropping off of me. Even though it was late, I had to eat. I went to the refrigerator and dished up some homemade split pea soup — one of my comfort foods. I took my cup of soup, and a small glass of wine into the office. Baba, our neurotic five-year-old shelter rescue kitty, joined me and purred as I sat on the sofa, with my rules of the road book open. Tears welled up in my eyes. I forced them back. My fear of failure was mounting. There was no time to deal with it, much less than acknowledge it. I had to learn my material. I scanned the pages again, whispering out loud. An hour later, I crawled into bed.

Thursday arrived. The alarm went off. I dragged myself out of bed. I dry brushed my skin, a routine I've had for over 20 years. With a natural bristle brush, I stroked my body from toe to head in short sections, always moving in direction of the heart. In some areas, such as the buttocks, I use circular motions. It stimulates the lymph system, removes dead skin, and gives me a shot of energy, much like a strong cup of coffee. This morning it felt like a weak cup. I stumbled to the kitchen, flicked on the coffeepot. In the past few days I realized this is one habit that I would definitely have to kick. It's one thing being a passenger and needing to call for privacy, but it's another to be the guide, especially a woman guide and dropping your drawers in the wide open spaces. I vowed to remove it from my diet, but realized now was not the time. I needed all the help I could get to keep my eyes open and my senses alert.

New clients arrived at the breakfast table — a man and his son from Colorado. His wife, suffering from cancer, would come down later I was told. The men eagerly headed to the Bay with Scott, and I headed for my books. I took my coffee and made my way to the alcove on the second floor of our home. It's a sacred space, where I read, do my yoga, and workout on the treadmill. Normally I enjoy the sights from this perch. Out the large window in the den, I look out over the ranch land across the Arroyo. From here I witness the growing population of javelina and wild hogs trampling along the banks and watch the birds soar by at near eye level. Outside the other window looking into our front yard, I overlook the anaqua tree, a native species with thick dark green leaves, fragrant tiny white blossoms, and yellow changing to orange berries. It is a favorite stopping place for sparrows, mockingbirds, and butterflies. Across the street, I view the seemingly endless shrimp ponds. But this morning, I failed to note any of it. I opened my books, and shut out the rest of the world. Two hours later, after one round of review, I stood up and stretched. I did a few asanas, and retreated to the bedroom. I could barely keep my eyes open, and by 9:00 I already needed a nap.

I could only hover. Hovering, to me, is like an altered state of consciousness. I was not really sleeping, I was not meditating, but I wasn't entirely in my body. It's a welcome state when I'm both mentally and physically exhausted. I was roused by the doorbell, and I jumped up, expecting my client for breakfast. Instead I saw the back of the UPS man moving away from the door. I looked at the package, noticing that it was the galleys for *Sacred Encounters with Mary*, Scott's book he's revised for a Texas publisher. Our new life had given rise to new energy for old projects that weren't given their proper due. I was excited, but just couldn't take the time to do more than open the envelope and look at the font and the layout. This was an unusual response for someone who has spent over 15 years in the publishing business as both a writer and an editor. I laid it on the desk and went back to the bedroom, this time to pray and meditate.

I needed some sacred time. Settling into the silence, I felt a blanket of peace envelop me. A subtle energy began to course through my veins. Despite my lack of sleep and the juggling of my current responsibilities, I knew I was doing exactly what I was being called to do. Just as I felt nudged in making the commitment to sea school, I felt supported during my studies. The path had been cleared. Our clients had been supportive and actually excited about my new adventure. They eagerly pitched in with dinner and regularly inquired as to my progress.

My son also accepted new challenges — a job marketing Chrysler vehicles. He withdrew from school and left town the week before my studies began. He took a big step not only for himself, but also for me. He'd be traveling around the country for a year. It was a relief. He'd been challenging. Being the only family members close by, he relied on us for much of his emotional and at times financial support. It was often difficult for me not to let the intensity of his life negatively affect my own.

My grandmother looked at him when he was about nine months old and said, "That child has the devil shining out of his eyes." He has a big heart, but he's got a lot of lessons to learn. Anyone around him feels it and is affected by it. As his mother, it has been difficult to watch him fall on his knees, which he's done several times. But it has been harder to support him unconditionally, or perhaps better put co-dependently. I've spent precious amounts of my life energy worrying about Pete and his choices. I have had to remind myself that they are his choices and there's nothing I can do about any of them. I had my own choices to make and now I was being blessed with the psychic and physical space to do so. It has been over a week, and he was really enjoying his new job and his new friends. And I was beginning to enjoy my newly found freedom.

The doorbell rang. My guest arrived. She offered to take her food back to her room. Initially it sounded like a good idea.

"I do have to study," I said to her.

Suddenly I realized that giving this woman a little time out of my day was what I was being asked to do to be of greater service to God. "I have a few minutes. Please sit here." I nodded toward the table.

She looked relieved. I began warming her eggs and pouring her juice. She talked. I listened. She told me of her ovarian cancer which had gone undiagnosed for two years. I saw the bitterness in her eyes. I probably would be bitter too. She used to fly fish — before she got sick. Now she hasn't the energy, and she's left on the bank while her husband and son take to the water. It was what they need to help them through the demands her illness places on them. She has taken up painting, flowers in particular. It seemed to bring her great joy. After making up a lunch plate for her, I joined her at the table with my coffee. We talked of our children.

After awhile, I felt the energy draining from me. I rose and in doing so signaled the end of my availability, with as much love and grace as I could muster. It has been what I've had to do with Pete, even my friend Jane, in order to preserve the time and energy I have complete this current goal.

The hardest part of sea school was making the time to study. For me this meant protecting my time against any unnecessary intrusions. I forewarned everyone, such as my friends and children, that I would be unavailable for anything but dire emergencies. I'd made the commitment and I intended to see it through. I didn't even feel particularly apologetic to our clients for not being present at dinner. By stating my intentions aloud, I felt everyone come into alignment with my decision.

I studied for another four hours that day, completing 50 sample questions. I missed 10 out of 50. It wasn't good enough.

Scott came home from a tough day of guiding. I had that "caught in the headlights" look. He kissed me. "This isn't a mark of whether you're good or not. You're a good person, even if you don't pass the test."

Tears welled up in my eyes. "I didn't realize until now, how important this is to me." I sighed. "I want to do this and I want to do well."

"Then you will."

Zen master Shunryu Suzuki, who authored the well-known book, *Zen Mind, Beginner's Mind*, said, "We should find out the meaning of our effort before we attain something. It is not after enlightenment that we find its true meaning. The trying to do something in itself is enlightenment."

I was truly becoming enlightened about myself in this process.

I prayed the rosary during my drive. I felt Mary watching over me. I prayed to Jesus for all the support I needed, and he too made his presence known. Pat drilled us for an hour. I knew more than I realized. My confidence rose several notches. Test time. Rick, the other fly fisher, whizzed through, and left early. I assumed he passed. The plan was, we'd test, and if we failed, we'd review and retest immediately before going onto the next session. My palms were sweaty. I was in silent competition with Rick, who merely symbolized all the male authorities who dominated this field. I wanted to prove that I could do this work just as well as any guy. Yet I was constantly trying to convince myself that passing or failing wasn't the issue. It was my commitment to the process that mattered most.

I surveyed the last few days. I'd done all I could to ensure my success. I ruthlessly protected my time. I took a deep breath and returned to the questions. My friend Dawn flashed into my mind. We've known each other since grade school, and she often remarked how schoolwork came so easily to me. I'd ace exams without even studying. She had no idea how much I've studied for this. I reminded myself to email her when after I've gotten through this process.

I finished and reviewed my answer key to make sure I didn't leave any blank. I refused to go back and reread each question. After taking my exam to Pat, I retreated to my seat and stared out the window, tapping my feet. Occasionally, I glanced in his direction, not really daring to watch him grade my paper. He looked up and smiled. I went to his desk. One wrong.

"Way to go," he said.

A wave of relief washed over me, and a wide grin formed on my lips. I mumbled thank you, gathered my things, and headed to the car. Even before I put the key in the ignition, I called Scott.

"I passed!"

"Congratulations."

"I got just one wrong."

"Does this make you as smart as me?" he asked, alluding to the fact that he'd gotten only one wrong on this particular section.

"It means I'm over my first hurdle. I'm coming home." I drove home, saying thanks aloud to all my silent supporters. Then I dialed my daughter's number. Suddenly I realized how much I'd missed talking to her. Over the past year, we talked more like friends than parent/child. It's been a pleasant development to our relationship. I know that one day the same will come to be with Pete. "Shana, I passed."

"Does this mean I can call you Captain Mom now?" Her reaction ranked right up there with passing the test. My children had witnessed me at my weakest during their early childhood years. I was grateful that I could show them a better side of me, one which would give them hope during their inevitable dark nights as they matured.

I chuckled. "Not yet. One down, three to go."

Friday, I had the day pretty much to myself. We didn't have any homework since the plan was to start a new section that evening. We whizzed through it. Saturday arrived, and I headed to class early.

"I guess this is hump day," I said to Pat. "We're halfway there."

He grinned. His style of teaching had been efficient and pleasurable. He made it easy to learn a lot of material in a short amount of time. After a quick review, we took the test. I aced it. *Yes!*

I returned home early enough to take a two-hour nap, a leisurely bath, and enjoy a fine glass of wine on the back porch with my husband before dinner. I watched as the seagulls headed back to the Bay for their nightly roost. In the distance a great blue heron squawked his indignation toward the Harris hawk practicing kamikaze dives over the heron's head, most likely to be an annoyance. Simple pleasures. I relished them.

Monday night we received our navigation charts. Ironically, it was of the Chesapeake Bay — our old stomping grounds.

I unrolled it, and became instantly excited. Visions of large ships going to sea, Rudee Inlet, and the Chesapeake Bay Tunnel flitted through my mind. Something stirred deep inside me as I looked at the chart. I yearned to soak it up — the symbols, the numbers — all of it.

Scott marveled at my genuine interest in the subject matter. No matter how hard the schedule had been on me, particularly juggling clients and studying, I was really enjoying myself — and I wanted to learn more. Even when I felt most challenged, I was aware of an inner strength that supported my genuine desire to see this process through with success.

The night was long and intense. Measuring accurately was my most difficult task, and remained my weak point for the next few days. One little slip and my answers were off by enough of a margin that made an educated guess at the multiple-choice options impossible.

Tuesday morning Pat called. He had an emergency and had to cancel class. He asked how I was doing. I said, "Fine. I got it." I hadn't yet sat down to study, but my plan was to spend the afternoon at the kitchen table doing the problems.

"Call me if you have any questions," he said.

I worked on a couple of problems and didn't do too well. I decided to take the evening off, looking at the cancellation of class as a gift. Even though our fly fishing business was first and foremost on our agenda, Scott continued his psychotherapy practice on a part-time basis three evenings a week. When he finished with his counseling client, we headed to the porch. Our time was our own, at least for the night. Scott and our friend Skipper planned on fishing the next day. He asked if I wanted to go. I made a noise of disgust. "I have too much to do. I have to shop and I have to study," I said. Suddenly, I felt guilty for taking the evening off.

Wednesday, I rose early with Scott. We meditated, and Skipper arrived. I laid out my character reference on the table, which he had agreed to sign during a previous conversation.

"I can't sign that until you prove to me you can handle the boat," Skipper chuckled.

I felt wounded. With as much grace as I could muster, I

rode with Scott and Skipper to the launch. In truth I wanted to hide and have a good cry. But I had to bring the trailer and the car back in order to go to town.

My first pass into the driveway was a failure. I couldn't get the trailer to do what I wanted it to do. I gave up, extremely frustrated, and pulled straight in. My intention was to unhook the trailer and push it to the grass. I couldn't budge it; no matter how hard I tried. I cussed and gave it one more heave. My back wrenched. I cussed again, and looked up at the sky. "Why do you have to make things so difficult for me?" I felt that every added hurdle was impeding my plan to study.

I hooked the trailer to the Rodeo and I pulled out of the driveway. I then backed the trailer into the driveway, taking a few minutes to get it in exactly the right place. I got out of the car, feeling much like a chastised teenager, embarrassed at my earlier outrage for having to do something I just didn't want to do. I had accomplished this feat, which had previously felt insurmountable — and with little more than 15 minutes worth of effort. Best of all, I'd broken through one of my self-imposed limitations.

I rushed around, preparing to go to the store. We had new guests arriving that day. I readied their room, putting drinks and snacks inside. I left them a note on the main door, just in case they arrived before I returned from the store.

Then I left Skipper a note. "I'll take you for a ride if you're here when I get home." I put my character reference back in my folder and picked up my study materials. Then I continued with my preparations to leave the house.

At one point I stubbed my toe on a chair in the den. I sat down and cried. Sam put his snout up between my hands and sniffed. He didn't understand. I realized I didn't have time to cry, but the tears wouldn't stop. I was extremely tired, and Skipper's remark hurt like hell. It hit a big button. I searched my psyche as to why.

His support was important to me. His remark also reminded me of a comment my father made to me many years ago, when I got all A's on my report card. He asked why I didn't get A+'s. I was crushed and rushed to my room in a fit of tears.

I pulled myself together and headed to the door. Sam followed expectantly, and I reluctantly agreed to let him join me. I felt drained as I walked through the store and the process of selecting the food I needed seemed to take forever. At some point in the dairy section, I decided that I was not going to take Skipper for a ride that day. His support just was not that important. My priorities were to get ready for my guests and to study. I'd get another character reference. I returned to the car with a full grocery cart. I opened the door, and immediately noticed that Sam had chewed the seat belt. I scolded him, but realized it was as much my fault as his. I'd been gone a long time. He was a good dog, but no doubt got very bored waiting for me to rejoin him. The day just wasn't getting any better.

As I was driving home, Scott called. He sensed right away that something was wrong. I told him how Skipper's remark had hurt. I began to cry. "I'm so tired of working so hard. I'm not even going to get to do my homework. I gotta go." I hung up. Usually I liked to talk to Scott, share with him and process my feelings. Today, I just didn't have the energy. I was drained not only from all the studies, but my other responsibilities as well.

Our housekeeper had taken a steady job in January, during our slow season when we couldn't provide her with many hours. I had resorted to doing all of her duties myself. The task of finding a replacement seemed daunting. Maria knew the routine and what we expected. We trusted her. Our lodge was not only our business; it was first and foremost our home. I didn't want just anyone coming into my space whom I couldn't trust implicitly. My resistance to bringing someone new into the business was taking a heavy toll on me.

Scott greeted me in the driveway. He had a full morning himself. After flounder fishing with Skipper, he mowed the lawn. We unloaded the car together. I sobbed as I walk to and fro. Sherry, our neighbor, was out mowing her lawn. I turned my head, hoping she wouldn't see my tears.

Scott joined me in the kitchen as I unpacked the groceries. "I dunked the digital today," he told me.

I look stunned and shook my head. The water is a grave-yard for things like cameras and keys. "We're not having a very good day, are we?"

I glanced at the clock, realizing I would never get to study.

He turned the subject to Skipper. "His remark just reflects your doubt in your abilities to be out on the water with clients."

"I know." Truth was, while I may have put in a great deal of sea time, I hadn't driven the boat a lot, particularly from dock to dock. There's a lot to know and to learn. I had a good deal of fear about going out there alone.

"He may have been joking," he added. "You know how he is."

I nodded. Skipper has a wry sense of humor. He used to frighten me. Now, most days, I can match his wit with friendly zings of my own. Today was not one of them. I took his comment to heart.

"You need to call him," Scott urged.

"That's not my priority right now."

I finished my kitchen chores in barely enough time to head to class. I hopped in the car and after a few miles, I pulled the cell phone from my purse and called Skipper. He didn't answer, nor did I leave a message.

I entered the classroom, barely taking note of the beautiful afternoon on South Padre Island. Our classroom overlooked the causeway to the west, and some evenings we witnessed remarkable sunsets. During many of our breaks, I marveled at the fact that I was living the life I'd always dreamed of. I had my house on the water, and I was able to spend a lot of time out in nature.

Class began. Pat mentioned other classes he wanted to teach, such as advanced charting and plotting, plus a section on weather. I mentally shouted my enthusiasm. But first, I had to get through the first section. The night was long and intense. My eyes hurt, and so did my back. Bending over the tables exacerbated the muscle pull I inflicted upon myself that morning while trying to move the trailer. We learned more new material, adding to my mental confusion. By the end of the

View from the porch, looking over the Arroyo Colorado

evening, I was ready to be home. I barely had enough energy to drive, and in a manner so unlike me, I waited to call Scott until after I crossed the causeway and leaving Port Isabel.

"Did you call Skipper?" he asked.

"Yeah."

"He called here accusing me of not leaving a message. I told him it was probably you."

"What else did he say?"

"You know that's not my place. You need to talk to him." Scott hated triangulation.

I was silent.

"Okay, he was joking." I felt relieved. My father was too about my grades. I took such comments to heart, because of my lousy lack of self-esteem. I've tried hard over the years to keep it at bay, but it always finds a way to weasel into my psyche when I'm overtired.

Thursday arrived and it was a beautiful morning for fishing. I was envious of our clients as they left the dock with Scott. It had been so long since I'd been out on the water. I reminded myself, first things first. I'd be done with this course in just two more days.

I called Skipper, while sweeping the floors. I admitted that I took his comment seriously.

"I should have signed it yesterday. It just slipped my mind," he said.

We talked about the course, and I told him that I was really enjoying it.

"You never know when some rich folks might hire you to drive their boat to the Caribbean."

I lit up. "That sounds tough to take."

"I've done it, and it's not half bad," he added.

We made a plan to meet later in the day on my way to class. Then I went back to my chores. I prepared much of dinner right after breakfast, and tended to other household chores, like washing the filthy windows. Dog nose prints of all shapes and sizes covered the lower half of the patio doors thanks to Sam and the girls, his beagle friends from next door. The morning whizzed by. I did yoga, showered, and pulled out my charts. I stared at them for over an hour. None of it made any sense. At 2:00 I had another good cry. Then I realized that I was due for my period by week's end. I'd done a lot of crying in the last few days. I was usually more resilient, but the stress of sea school had sent me over the edge. I returned to my charts and called Pat. "I'm lost."

He walked me through a problem. "I got it. I think." I hung up and did a problem, then another, and another. They were all correct. I was confident that I did indeed have it. I called Pat and left him a message.

At 4:00 I rolled up my charts and packed up my books. I went back to the kitchen to finish dinner. I left Post-its on the range hood and on the refrigerator for Scott, so he'd have no problem finding the menu components. I also sketched out a step-by-step list, reassuring him that he'd spend no more than ten minutes finishing dinner. He hadn't come off the Bay by the time I left, so I had no cell phone for my ride. I was relieved. I was forced into silence. I needed the time to pray, feeling less than confident as the time for the test fast approached.

Ten questions. We had to get seven out of ten right. We started with another quick review and by 7:00 we started the exam. Tom, the shrimper, whizzed through. Usually, he was the last at the desk on exam nights. With a family and a full-time job, he barely had time to study. I felt a lot of empathy for him. He beamed when Pat gave him the results. Rick finished next, several minutes behind Tom.

"Done?" Pat asked.

"As I'm ever gonna be." I sensed the doubt in his voice.

All of my competitive feelings had disappeared. Instead we bonded, the four of us, over the last week and a half. We shared family stories and fishing stories. We laughed, and we commiserated. I felt like one of the guys.

Rick left. I looked up at Pat. "Well it's no surprise who'd be the last to be sitting here tonight, is it?" I said.

He chuckled and went about his business, leaving the room to go to his office. I envisioned having to take this section of the test again. It had been more difficult for me than I felt comfortable to admit even to myself.

Pat returned just as I finished my last question. I literally guessed at two answers because there was no other way for me to answer them. I drew a blank just looking at the words. He scored the test in front of me. I was barely breathing as he reviewed the answer key. The tension mounted to an unbearable level. I wanted to run, to hide — back to my cave and my comfort zone. He looked up — again smiling. I made it with just two wrong. I breathed a gigantic sigh of relief, and the weight lifted off my shoulders.

The ride home passed slowly, peacefully. I said prayers of thankfulness the entire way, mostly out loud. I was beaming inside and out. Scott was roaming around the yard when I pulled into the driveway. He'd been gassing the boat and tidying up the porch.

"You didn't call." He sounded concerned.

"I didn't have the phone." I replied.

He chuckled. "I forgot." He looked at me expectantly.

"I passed."

He lit up and leaned over to kiss me. "Congratulations."

"Thanks." I stumbled into the house exhausted, ready for the day to be over.

"Do you want to eat?"

I shook my head. "I'm just too tired." I set the table for breakfast, made coffee for the morning, and headed for the shower. I fell into bed and was asleep almost immediately. In what seemed like an instant the alarm rang again.

Friday. I stayed home and caught up on office work and a little more housework. I read something spiritual. I did yoga. I napped. Boat safety and handling were scheduled to begin that evening. I spent a bit of time with our client's wife. I had such little contact with anyone over the last two weeks, even myself. I was numb to my feelings on one hand, and yet amazingly intuitive and focused on the other. Five o'clock arrived and once again I was off for my 50-minute ride to the Island. Class ran later than usual, adding to my fatigue. I dragged myself back home, with my back aching and my throat showing signs of tenderness. I took a hit of Vitamin C and a handful of vitamins, prior to repeating my nightly ritual.

New clients greeted me in the morning: a father and a son. They arrived early for breakfast, which was unusual. Most clients sauntered in well past the set time, often delaying their departure from the dock. But this morning everything seemed to be in flow. I had to be in class by 8:00. The plan was to review and then test. Following a short break, we were to take First Aid. All fell into place. I finished the test and had just 5 wrong out of 60. We were allowed 15 incorrect answers. I made it. I turned around to leave. Pat called me back. He handed me my certificate. I beamed from ear to ear, and suddenly I felt like crying again. But this time out of pride, not frustration and weariness. I did it. I made it through sea school! Only the formalities of submitting my paperwork stood between me and my status as a fully-fledged captain.

A sense of pride in myself that I hadn't felt in a very long time coursed through my veins. On a practical level, I made it through a very tough course. Skipper later told me it took him three times to pass the test. He wasn't alone. I heard similar tales.

On a psychological/spiritual level, I worked through a very deep issue. Over the years, I let my sense of over responsibility to other people's issues, goals, and agendas get in the way of my own. I witnessed my mother do the same. With an over committed schedule she never finished nursing school; she instead became ill. Of late, she complained that she could never get her own house in order, yet she tended to the church office and the homes of several folks who spend their weekends in the country. My hometown, where my parents still reside, is just two hours north of New York City, a haven for overstressed city dwellers. Everyone loves her; she's become indispensable. But I've often wondered will she ever do anything for herself before there's nothing left even if she loves being of service?

On Monday, Scott and I planned to spend the day celebrating my captaincy and attending to some errands in town. It was my first real day off in over two weeks. Before we left the doorbell rang. As I approached the door, I saw my neighbor Sherry with her back to the door. Her husband, Rex, stood to the side. I opened the door and she turned around holding a cake that said, "Capt. Kathy" on the top. I was speechless, and flattered. I received nothing but support from everyone — friends, family, clients, and acquaintances — but mostly from Scott. I wasn't the only one to have pulled double duty these last few weeks; he had as well.

I showed him the cake. "This is your BA," he said, referring to my being just ten credits shy of my academic degree.

"Yeah, it is. I saw this one through to the end."

I had let the chaos of my past life get in the way of my goals. Now it seemed too late — and in many ways unnecessary — to pursue my academic badge of honor. However, my latest endeavors held a far deeper meaning. I broke through a self-defeating pattern and hoped that my efforts would somehow overtly or covertly influence my children to break through their own.

Aye, Aye Captain

June 1, 2002. My inaugural trip onto the Lower Laguna Madre as Captain Kathy. I awoke at 4:23 a.m., and forced myself not to lie in bed thinking that I must get back to sleep. Instead I prayed, and dozed a bit before rising at 5:15.

We had five guests at the Inn that weekend, including two gentlemen from California, who were to be my charter for the day. They'd been out with Scott the two previous days and had some success thus far. Three others were to go with Scott on their boat. I downed a protein shake as I gathered my gear and provisions. I was eager to be on the water. I wanted it to be over, at least the initial plunge. I wasn't overly nervous but there was a cloud of anxiety that hung over me. My mood stayed light, despite the added worry of a motor that wasn't functioning optimally after its most recent service call.

It was nearing the time to leave. I went back to my room and finished dressing. I tucked my rosary in my pocket, grabbed my coat and my fanny pack, and took a deep breath. It was show time. I felt cloaked by the Divine.

I stopped at the door long enough to give Scott a kiss.

"Good luck. We'll stay in touch." He said, standing in the doorway, holding his coffee cup in hand.

I mumbled something barely audible, and left the house in somewhat of a fog. I wandered toward the boat alone, Scott's presence by my side noticeably missing. I glanced toward the boat. Time seemed to slow down and every nuance of my surroundings amplified. The boat was firmly attached to the ramp with the rope. Definitely not in launching position. For a moment, I felt disappointed that Scott hadn't lowered it completely into the water for me. But just as quickly, I realized he really couldn't have if I was to fully own my experience.

I put my gear on board, and returned to the bow to shove it further down the ramp. It was quite a stretch for my short arms, and I had to be careful not to fall head first into the Arroyo. That wouldn't have been a good way to start the day.

Dan and Peter joined me on the dock at 6:30, the sun barely peeking over the horizon. I stored their gear, including Dan's video camera, trying not to imagine the cost of his equipment and what could happen on the water. I didn't want to be responsible for tossing him and it overboard. I settled them into the seat in front of the console, and started the motor. We had a sticky beginning. I didn't get the boat far enough off the ramp for it to disengage when I put it in reverse. I had to get off, give it a little heave-ho, and then climb back aboard. I backed the boat out and then headed down the Arroyo. I was tentative, and it took longer than necessary to get the boat onto plane, where it rode comfortably and effortlessly on the surface of the water. I said a quick prayer. I asked that Christ's light surround us and protect us on our journey throughout the day, a prayer that I repeated often as the day progressed. There was always a noticeable essence that surrounded me with this prayer, something I found very comforting.

Having discussed all the possible options with Scott, I decided to go into Rattlesnake Bay in hopes that the redfish would be tailing. Tailing trout were an added bonus I also hoped for.

The mouth of the Arroyo was calm, as it usually is in the early morning hours. The wind was still less than 10 mph. The sun was just beginning to make its presence known over the horizon, subtly illuminating Bird Island in front of us. I scanned the horizon. There were few boats out, and I felt confident that I would be able to stick with Plan A.

The entrance to Rattlesnake is marked by a weather station. Scott's words about obstacles and shallow areas ran through my head. There's so much to remember when boating the Lower Laguna. Other than channel markers and the spoil islands, there are no road signs or definitively marked paths to travel along. Stakes mark some of the submerged items which could knock out the lower unit on a motor, rendering the boat disabled, and possibly causing injury to passengers if we went off plane suddenly. These stakes are usually made of white PVC, typically used in plumbing applications. Of late however, night fishermen have been littering the Bay with PVC stakes, on which to tie their boats. Unfortunately, instead of keeping boaters from hazards, they are now becoming hazardous. Absolute attentiveness is necessary at all times.

As a passenger in my earlier days on the water, I did little more than notice the flora, fauna, and other aspects of the environment. Now I had no choice but to start an encyclopedia in my mind of shallow areas and obstacles. Remembering it all was crucial to the safety of my clients, my boat, and myself. I regret not paying more attention, but realize I didn't really have to up until the last few months.

Before becoming the spiritual head of Siddha Yoga, Gurumayi Chidvilasananda served as interpreter for Swami Muktananda and had been his disciple since her childhood. One day he requested that she learn English in order to be his interpreter for an impending tour. She lamented that he did not require that she learn sooner. He explained that without the necessity to learn English, she would not have readily done so.

It was now a necessity that I learn everything I could about the Bay and remember it. During our personal times on the water, I drilled Scott about each area we boated. I observed my surroundings with the eye of an eagle, soaking in every detail. I studied maps of the area. Slowly my encyclopedia was forming.

I rounded Channel Marker 4 and kept my eyes peeled for any obstacles I passed through the center of the mouth into Rattlesnake Bay and veered left after passing some grassy areas. Grass will block the water intake, causing the motor to overheat. I preferred a planned shut down and take off, to one precipitated by a problem.

As I rounded the south side of Rattlesnake Island, and came to a stop a hundred yards or so away from the duck blind, I realized that this was the area that Scott brought me to first during my early days as a fly fisher. Subconsciously I had come full circle.

As a guide, I was about to deepen my relationship with the Mother Lagoon, and while I never expect to know her completely, I will come to know her differently. This day marked the end of my exploring simply as an angler. My explorations as a guide were beginning.

Oblivious to their participation in this moment in history, Dan and Peter readied their rods, while I scanned the horizon for tails. It was quiet. Not even a mullet jumped. I felt like the cove, tucked into the southern point of the island might be a good option. I suggested I move closer so they didn't have to wade far. It was too early in the day for a hefty workout. I raised the engine, tilted the motor in, and turned the motor all the way to the right, before accelerating. The first roll, or revolution, didn't bring us up on plane. I held back. I didn't give it enough gas. I hedged. I was going for a second, and the heat alarm went off. I put the boat in neutral and smoke poured out the engine. It didn't look good. My mind reeled with all sorts of possibilities. I hated the thought of being stranded just minutes after the day began.

I left the motor running, allowing the water to continue flowing through it, and thus cooling it down. The smoke dissipated, but I was far from calm. The alarm ceased, signaling that I could safely move the boat. Not wanting to chance another failed attempt, I putted to the cove. Once we were close, I shut off the motor and Peter and Dan commenced fishing. In the meantime my cell phone rang. It was Scott checking in. I was relieved. He assured me the smoke was most likely from the motor oil he spilled on it the night before while gassing up. Then we talked about fish. He was at the Trout Bar with his clients and it was quiet there as well. We were biding time until the sun came up and we could move east. We had three hours ahead of us before the sun would be high enough in the sky to see fish beneath the surface of the water.

I scouted ahead of Dan and Peter, walking across Rattlesnake Island to the north. From there, I could see that the boats that were anchored near the entrance had left. There wasn't any action at all. I groaned. A guide's nightmare: No fish.

The weather had changed the day before, and we had a light norther blow through about midafternoon. It stirred up the fish, sending them to parts unknown. Upon hearing the forecast two days before, I knew it was going to be a difficult day. However, I was grateful it wasn't raining, nor blowing 20 mph out of the north. It was still less than ten, which was a plus. I rejoined Peter and Dan, and suggested we move to Channel Markers 41 and 43. If we were going to blind cast, it might as well be off the channel where the chances of snagging a fish would be increased.

They boarded and I got the boat up with ease, thankfully on the first turn so the earlier scenario wasn't repeated.

Channel Markers 41 and 43 are located south of Duncan's Channel. I had fished them a couple of weeks before with two lady clients, during our first teaching weekend of the season. There were fish, including several large trout, which taunted me, most likely knowing I did not have a rod in hand. There was also an interesting pass between two spoils that intrigued me.

We stopped first at Channel Marker 43, and I got out of the boat to set the anchor close to the channel. I sank up to my thighs on the first step. I knew that neither Dan nor Peter would want to get out there. I decided to move the boat to 41. There I found a firmer spot for Peter to stay in while he cast out into and along the channel. I reminded him that big trout sometimes skirt the edge of the channel, along the grass line. He used a small Clouser which is one of the most popular flies, that has caught more species than any other pattern. It has weighted eyes, with a bucktail wing. As it moves through the water, it effectively imitates a bait fish. This is about the only scenario, where we use weighted flies. Usually our venues are so shallow, that weight is unnecessary to sink the flies into the fish's sight window.

Dan stayed aboard and pulled out his video equipment. In addition to recording his own adventures for posterity, he professionally records videos for lodges. Upon seeing his work, we added our name to his list of ever-growing clients.

I sat back and had a snack, while watching the sights around me. Occasionally, I looked over my shoulder to the east to check out the clouds over the sand. Scott called me on the radio to inform me that they were heading to Duncan's Channel in hopes of finding fish. They too were biding time.

Parked along the edge of the channel, Dan, Peter, and I were quite a sight. Two Asian-American men — one fly fishing, the other with a video camera — and a chick at the helm. We were an anomaly. I smiled, remembering the rubbernecking that I witnessed in my earlier days wielding a fly rod on the Bay. Many a time I'd be standing along the Intracoastal, fishing the flats or the edge of the channel, and a boat would go by, with the guys aboard craning their necks. One such day I overheard one say, "That's a lady...and she's fly fishing!" I must have seemed like an apparition since I was alone and neither Scott nor our boat were in view.

Now they were checking out the lady fly-fishing guide and her clients. I never thought I'd be a pioneer. I guess the urge to conquer new vistas runs deep — either from my Native American ancestors or from my Irish ancestors who ventured to the new land.

Peter had no more than a bump from a flounder for all his efforts. He was a proficient caster, and could easily switch from right to left handed whenever he needed. It was a joy to watch. Casting can be such a beautiful art form.

We moved across the ICW to Channel Marker 42. We stayed for a short time, with no measurable success, other than Dan capturing some boat traffic for the video. I felt the urge to move east.

As I picked up the radio to call Scott, he called in for me. I took it as a good sign. We were in sync. They too were on the move, and heading east, having no luck at their own location.

For the next four hours, we hopscotched various locations from Land's End to Grand Bahama, names assigned to certain areas on the sand by our friend Fred. Some location names are common knowledge; others are codes assigned by Fred, meant to protect sensitive areas from eavesdropping anglers.

Our clients had some success; Scott's had a couple of landed redfish and a chance at big trout. Mine scored with the lady-fish. Peter got out of the boat at one location and said, "I just want a ladyfish." He enjoyed their play the day before, and had yet to land one, since it broke off — a normal occurrence due to their abrasive mouths. He had another chance. A big red swam by him and he cast. A ladyfish came out of nowhere and danced away with his fly on the first strip. He groaned. I reminded him that he did say he wanted a ladyfish. "Now you need to ask for your redfish." It remained an elusive goal for him for the remainder of the day. The redfish were far and few between despite our best efforts to find them.

I continued to walk between Dan and Peter, spotting fish for them. A light wind blew from the northeast, so we were wading in a southwestwardly direction. We had rain for the first time in weeks just a couple of days before, and all the plants surrounding the Bay were flourishing from the dousing of fresh water. In the distance, I could see the vibrant new growth of the plants on the shoreline along Cullen's Bay.

We had waded quite a distance. I checked my watch and then told the guys, I would retrieve the boat, and float back to them so they wouldn't have to retrace their steps. I turned and was instantly mesmerized by the eastern view. The sky was beautiful blue with big puffy clouds. The clouds and the salty sand dunes on Padre Island melded together. It seemed sur-real, like something out of a Spielberg movie. I felt so blessed. I fingered my rosary and silently prayed. I was mindfully in the moment, completely aware of my surroundings, my clients, and myself. As I shuffled my feet, I occasionally glanced close by for any stingrays.

Two weeks earlier, during our first teaching weekend of the new season, I was in the Mudhole coaching clients as they made their way toward a large pod of tailing redfish. It was early evening and the birds were working over pods of redfish. We chose one in the southwest corner as our target. Fred and Scott remained aboard the boats, poling them behind us. Our clients ranged in experience from first time fly rodders to freshwater enthusiasts. One woman had considerable saltwater experience. But none had fished the Lower Laguna.

It seems that no matter how much experience someone has, there are fine points to fishing this fishery that need to go heeded if success is to be more than a dream. It's likely the case no matter where you fish, which is why guides are important.

We warned our clients to walk up to the pod as quickly and stealthily as they could, but not to cast until they were in comfortable casting distance. Our words fell upon deaf ears. They flogged the water with their lines. I'm sure out of excitement. I've been there. But by doing so, the fish remained out of reach. The pod kept moving, their heads rooting the bottom, yet subtly aware of some distant disturbance. I was shouting instructions to the client who was the closest to the pod. "Don't cast until you get closer." I wanted to grab his rod to make him stop casting. But I was several yards from him, and I'm not sure he heard me — or was paying attention.

I took a step forward, watching him continue to flail the water. Then I felt a whap, whap, whap against my booty. Time stood still. I tried to convince myself that it was a crab, but knew otherwise as I felt a sharp prick below my ankle. I screamed and cussed, for which I later apologized. Our clients stopped casting briefly to look in my direction. My eyes went wide with disbelief as I waited for the pain. I'd been hit by a stingray. I asked the woman next to me to hold onto my jacket so I could lift up my foot to survey the damage. Since I was sinking and losing my balance, I couldn't get my booty off. All I saw was an area in the zipper seam that had been frayed by the barb. Scott came closer with the boat.

"What happened?"

"I got hit."

He looked horrified. "Are you sure?"

"Positive, but I'm okay." I walked around a bit. "It's not that bad." I continued to wait for the effect of the marine poison to take hold. But being the guide with a job to do, I went back to my task at hand, encouraging the two women who were closest to me to cast toward the bank for any straggling reds. With their fellow anglers continuing onward, the pod was in fast

A lone fly fisher casting to his prey on the East Side

retreat. Even a mad dash forward wouldn't guarantee that they'd have even one shot at the pod. Their only hope for a hook-up was a straggler or two outside of the group.

When it became obvious that the pod was breaking up and any hope for redfish was lost, I knew my job was over. I wandered over to our boat.

"Would you get out the meat tenderizer?" I asked Scott as I scooted onto the deck.

At that time I wasn't wearing any flat's booties with stingray protection. I pulled off my booty, a little afraid to look. About an inch below my ankle, an area about the size of a dime was swollen. In the center was a puncture wound, not big, but more than a pinprick. Thankfully, I'd just been grazed. Scott handed me the tenderizer and I made a paste and applied it.

When all our clients had reconvened at the boats, I put on my booty and went back to Fred's boat. He'd yet to get his captain's license, so I was riding in his boat to ensure our legality. I was so ready to be home.

We returned to the lodge and I excused myself for a hot

bath in order to soak my ankle. I was lucky. My reaction was little more than tingly toes later in the evening. A deep achy feeling in my ankle lasted about 24 hours. I knew it could have been much worse.

Since it was an experience I did not want to repeat, I vowed to remain conscious of my steps, knowing that the ante always rises if I don't learn my lessons the first time.

Back on the white sand, Scott and I conferred and decided that the daylight was waning and without a concentration of fish, the time would soon come for us to head home. We decided to try one more venue. At about 4:00 we headed north in hopes of finding a stash of reds before the light was all but gone. I followed Scott, hugging the sand until the prop started kicking up the bottom. I moved farther to the west and some distance behind him. All eyes were peeled for fish. At one point I saw a dozen reds scrambling.

"Did you see that?" I said pointing to the west.

Peter turned around, and said, "Yeah, they went that way." He was pointing to the east. Both of us looked shocked, mouths wide open with disbelief. Dan later admitted he was catching a brief nap while we boated, thus missing the most significant sighting of the day. We had blown through a nice school of reds that had been cloaked by the foot plus depth of the water, a typical spring/fall scenario when the high tides are in vogue. However, this year, the trend was continuing well past the time when we usually have shallower water, thus making finding fish more difficult.

I steered to the west and shut down a few yards away. As we floated along, we scanned the surface for nervous water. The fish were gone and we were disappointed to say the least. It had been the most fish we had seen all day. We continued our trek north, having lost sight of Scott and his guys. We also lost radio contact some while back. I was on my own again. There were no fish as far north as the Green Island Spoils— which lie to the east of Green Island. It is a natural island, not one created by dredging, which has been designated a sanctuary by the National Audubon Society — a non-profit organization whose mission "is to conserve and restore natural eco-systems, focusing on birds, other wildlife, and their habitats for the benefit of humanity and the earth's biological diversity."

I had to turn around. The gas gauge was hovering just under a quarter of a tank. I retraced my steps angling more south-west, in hopes of finding those fish again. I came to the south side of Bird Island, near the mouth of the Arroyo, and set down. We had two options — to go in or to wait until the bird action started. I tried the radio once again, this time noticing that it had mysteriously changed channels on its own. I reset the channel to 78, and radioed Scott. He came through loud and clear. They were at the Trout Bar.

"How about meeting us at our favorite place?" he asked.

I smiled. "So you want to go to the Mudhole." I had no aversion to going back, despite my stingray encounter. I clearly knew it was my own fault, and while I was a bit more cautious and a little jumpier, I would not be kept from the water.

Peter and Dan's faces lit up. They'd witnessed the birding action the evening before. It is an exciting sight — churning water beneath laughing gulls; red tails waving in wild aban-don; shrimp fleeing for their lives from the reds, only to be caught midair by the birds.

"You go in first and check it out. We'll meet you there," Scott said.

We boated up the ICW, passing Skipper and his clients in the Flounder Hole, on the west side of the channel, just north of the mouth of the Arroyo. All of us were resorting to drastic measures that day to put clients on fish. Scott heard other guides pleading to each other for some insight. No one had any. Mother Nature had all fooled. The Mudhole was our last hope.

I pulled into the mouth of the muddy lagoon and circled to the left, going far back into the northwest corner. There were no birds working, just a few making some fly-bys in hopes of some action. We circled around back to the entrance, shut down, and rooted the birds on.

"Come on guys, find us some fish," I said. By this time, we were getting a little giddy from lack of sleep and a lot of sun.

Scott radioed that he would check out Peyton's, since nothing was happening in the Mudhole. Dan videoed a Great Egret and a first year ibis as we waited. We all chatted. Peter and Dan were easy clients and fun to be around.

We were nearing twelve hours on the water, and I had held up better than I feared. My anxiousness was but a memory. I was about to finish my maiden voyage as a captain. I had broken the ice. I didn't have to worry about this first day ever again.

"Captain Kathy, come in. Do you read me?"

I smiled, realizing that there were folks monitoring the radio waves hearing for the first time my name broadcast over the network. The word was out. There's a new kid in town. The song had been going through my head on and off all day. I responded. "I read you."

"Nothing happening. It's time to go in. We'll wait for you at the mouth of the Arroyo." Scott signed off, as he sped down the channel.

I watched as a tug pushing a long barge made its way down the ICW. It passed the mouth of the Mudhole just as I was up on plane. I entered the channel and scanned my options. Ideally, I needed to stay upwind of the barge, in case the motor went out. Barges suck the water off the flats, and in turn can pull a disabled boat under it. It's not a scenario I wished to ever experience. If you are upwind, chances of blowing to shore and away from danger are greatly increased. As we continued onward, I noticed that the space between Skipper's boat and the barge was minimal. I aborted my plan and crossed the ICW behind the barge, and sped along its port side, clearing it and Bird Island quickly. I entered the mouth of the Arroyo, where Scott and his charges awaited. We followed them on our homeward journey, leaving them at the Adolph Thomae Park launch. Dan, Peter, and I continued onward to our home dock. One more challenge to go — docking the boat on our ramp — on the first shot.

I looked for my neighbors' telltale dead palm, which stands in their backyard like a totem pole. I made a wide approach and aimed straight toward the ramp, careful to keep the motor straight and enough speed so the current didn't sweep us into my neighbors' dock. I said another prayer. The Curlew went up on the ramp with ease. I shut off the motor and jumped off to tether it to the cleat. I breathed a sigh of relief. I'd completed my first charter, losing neither equipment nor person overboard.

It takes a special boat to navigate these waters — a flats boat. Scott and I are the proud owners of a NewWater Boatworks Curlew — the ultimate fly fishing machine. The maker, Tim Clancey of San Antonio, is an artist. He expects nothing but the best from himself or his boats, making them a perfect match for the Lower Laguna. With a 90 horsepower motor, the Curlew floats in less than six inches of water, and we can start up in water that is about nine inches deep, even on a firm bottom. Best of all it's comfortable for our clients, and provides us with a smooth, dry ride. And we have plenty of storage for all of our gear.

Dan and Peter gathered their belongings, as I set about clearing clearing the ice chest. I went to the house, took off my long-sleeved shirt, said hello to Diggory, our latest addition to the

Kathy and Sam aboard the NewWater Boatworks Curlew

family. He'd been without company all day and greeted me with his squeaky meow.

After shedding my booties and my long-sleeved shirt, I returned to the boat and washed it off. I needed to bring the day full circle by cleaning the boat and pulling it all the way up on the ramp. With these tasks completed, I made my way back to the house cloaked by a wonderful sense of satisfaction.

Scott came in moments later. He walked up beside me and gave me a kiss. "I was very proud watching you out there today," he said.

"I'm glad you feel that way. I didn't want to disappoint you."

I was clearly in a new phase of my life. My nest was emptying, and I no longer held a burning desire to be self-sacrificing or overnurturing, which I had done for many years to win approval or avoid reproachment. I was redefining myself, coming to know myself in a different way. I was becoming more confident in myself and my motives. I was clearly making decisions from my heart, not my fears.

I had entered my midlife transition and was embracing new adventures. Joan Borysenko, Ph.D., author of *A Woman's Book of Life*, refers to this time in our mid- to late-forties as a "a second puberty." I was through bearing children, but I was far from over the hill. Borysenko says this time, "...can be the most powerful, exciting, and fulfilling half of a woman's life."

And I was beginning to see how. A lot had changed over the last few weeks. My son had been gone for two months. There was an ease in his voice that I hadn't heard in a long time, if ever. He said he was better than ever. I believed him. It was a pleasure to speak with him, and hear of his adventures around the country.

Our nest was indeed quieter. Our big black cat, Baba, moved onward as well, leaving us without warning of his departure. He was never a perfect fit, since he hated dogs, and came to us after living with an elderly woman with Alzheimer's. Our bustling lodge was more than he could handle. I suspected that he'd taken up with a single neighbor where he could be the center of attention.

Sam too was gone. He had taken his job to protect us more seriously than we needed, and began having difficulty distinguishing between guests and strangers. I left him in good hands, at a shelter that does not euthanize, with a treatise on the type of home that would be best for him. He needed a quieter stable environment, where as I wrote "the faces stay pretty much the same each day." It was a heartbreaking experience that reawakened some old memories.

In the days that followed my giving him away, I came to realize that his absence in my life was an answer to a prayer. I had requested the Divine to allow me to release anything that prevented me from experiencing balance in my life or didn't allow me to answer my true calling. I spent less time cleaning, and moved to my desk much earlier. And the days on the water weren't fraught with anxiety about who might come into the yard, or if we'd get back soon enough to let Sam out if he was in the house. Scott too had his sadness about losing Sam. But it was different from mine. Sam was the third lab that I had to give away over the course of the last 25 years, due to various circumstances. My dream dog, a big black lab was like apple pie and white picket fences are to some. Leaving Sam also reminded me very much of leaving my son to live with his father when I moved to Virginia Beach. The heartache was at times overwhelming. This time, however, I prayed for grace, for peace in my heart and my mind. I knew I had made the right decision now, as I did then. This time I was able to let go more easily. Occasionally the pain resurfaced briefly, but inwardly I knew that Sam was happy and safe.

My life had become like a blank journal. For the first time in over decades, I was unencumbered by children or pets that needed me to be vigilantly attentive to their needs. I could now attend to my own. I had more waters to explore, different species of fish to catch, and more clients to fish. I had so much more of my self to explore and so much more to write.

Renowned poet and novelist, Ursula Le Guin said, "It is good to have an end to journey towards, but it is the journey that matters in the end."

I was worrying less now about getting things done, about

obtaining a certain goal. I was beginning to trust the process — the journey — knowing when God wills it, doors would open and I would be in the right place at the right time. I needed only to have the courage to do my part and respond appropriately.

Some Call it Grace

June 5, 2002. Grandmother Trout remained elusive, showing herself to me of late when I had no rod in hand and clients to attend to. This morning Scott called me from the Bay. He'd gone out fishing, and I opted to stay home to put the finishing touches on this book.

"The Trout Bar was covered with trout. I have never seen so many," he said.

I groaned. I knew it. I felt her whispering to me. I spent five good hours in front of the computer screen. It was satisfying, very satisfying. Yet underneath the surface of my skin, I felt an eagerness and unsettledness. I walked outside and could smell the flats, the pungent sweet salty aroma distinctly associated with the spoil islands sprinkled around the Bay. Something deep inside of me that had no name stirred.

Scott came in about mid-day. He looked relaxed and at peace. He had hooked three trout, and all broke off. He went on to land three redfish in the Mudhole. I was happy for him. He needed to be alone with the Mother Lagoon. He too has a special relationship with her, one that needs tending to in solitude from time to time. I went outside to mow the lawn. From sitting so long, I had energy coursing through me that needed an outlet. The grass also badly needed a cutting, stemming from the rain we had just two days prior. Two hours later, sweaty and smelly beyond belief, I felt better. I was ready for a cool shower. Scott had a couple of counseling appointments and so we reconvened in early evening on the porch.

"I think we ought to go out in the morning for just a couple of hours," he said. He saw me hesitate. "We have a habit of stopping short, just before we're about to reach our goal." I knew he was referring to my quest for an IGFA women's world record speckled sea trout. I pondered his remark, knowing that it was so true. We had of late become vigilant against such a pattern, something that had in the past frequently affected our business, our fishing, and our writing.

"Is there gas in the boat?" I knew we had no extra in storage. I had gone to the Sanchez Bait Stand to buy $3.00 of gas to finish the lawn, and at premium prices. That meant we most likely had less than a gallon left over in the container.

"There's about a quarter of a tank," he said.

I knew we could get to the Trout Bar and back on that. "I can only go for a few hours. I have to get ready for the weekend, and I need to write."

"We'll be back by 9:00."

My heart skipped a beat. I was going fishing! After a quick pasta and clam sauce dinner, we readied our gear, checking our leaders and tippet, and attaching our fly of choice for our morning mission. I chose a white VIP, knowing it seemed to draw a trout's attention better than any other color we used. I dropped into bed at 10:30, relishing my prone position. I had little more than six hours sleep the night before. Five forty-five would come very quickly.

Scott woke up at 5:30, and I heard him stir and go out into the kitchen to turn on the coffee. I began my prayers, the usual ones I say before stepping foot from my bed. I asked for protection for my family and myself. I also asked that I be open and aware of God's will for me, and that I would respond appropriately.

Scott walked back into the room. "Don't you want to go fishing?"

"Yeah, I'm just finishing my prayers." I rolled over and swung my legs to the floor. I groaned aloud. Mowing the lawn was a heck of a full-body workout. We have just about a half an acre; much of it sloped and/or covered with thick carpet grass. When I'm mowing I usually envision more native landscaping, with stones and mulch replacing the suburban-like lawn. It would make things simpler and save on the water bill as well, but we've yet to have time to plant more than a few patches of drought-resistant native plants. The plan was to grab a cup of coffee in a traveling mug and go. Scott put bars, juice, and water on board while I dressed. We were on the dock in less than 15 minutes from the time my feet hit the ground. It was most likely a record.

Scott took the helm. I wasn't yet awake enough to drive. We got just a few feet from the dock, before he hesitated. "We have less than a quarter of a tank." I remembered the extra gas, and we pulled back to the dock. He ran for it, and I returned to the house for the cell phone — just in case we had to reach one of our friends ashore for a rescue mission. Gassed up, we took off. The eastern sky was barely turning light as we traveled down the Arroyo. Just past the park boat launch, a rain cloud let loose. I took over the helm while Scott searched for his coat. We drove the remainder of the way, about two miles, showered by raindrops.

As we approached the Trout Bar, we could see a single wader on the northern tip of the spoil bank. He posed no threat to our mission. Now back at the helm, Scott pulled off the channel just north of Channel Marker 203, shut off the motor, and secured the boat by staking the pole into the soft bottom. I began scanning the surface. I immediately saw one very large black triangle. Grandmother Trout was there. My heart skipped a beat. I was now wide awake and eager to get in the water.

"Would you mind if I changed your fly?" Scott asked. "This fly has a small gap hook on it. Chances of hooking would be better with a wider gap." He glanced at his rod. "I'll take this one off of mine." He then replaced my white foam-head VIP with a green-foam head VIP. I picked up my rod and was about to step off the boat, when he thought better his choice.

"I think white would be better."

I held my rod so he could grab the line. He dug in his pack for his fly box, and promptly found what he was looking for and tied it on. "I'm using a clinch knot." (Actually it was an improved clinch knot.)

Good thing, I thought. The last time he used a bowline knot when getting my gear ready it came loose and I broke off on a sizable red. I swore it was the last time I'd let him tie my flies on. For a moment I thought this might be some major cosmic trick to teach me to always take care of my own gear. He let the fly go, and it waved in the wind as I prepared once again to step off the boat. "Wait, what is that?" Scott pointed to the water not 10 feet from the boat. Two big trout were swimming by quickly. I franticly tried to whip out some line before they disappeared. "Backcast. Watch the rods behind you."

Two rods remained in the holders to my left, and Scott was to my right. I was boxed in. To top it off, my hands were wet and my line looked like a twisted pile of rubber bands coming off the reel. I made one cast and overshot them. One more pathetic cast later and the fish were all but a memory.

"That always happens when we don't have our gear ready," Scott said. I groaned silently. We had everything ready the night before — or so we thought. As I watched the trout swim away, I hoped they weren't the last I'd see.

I scooted off the edge of the boat and entered the water. Scott followed and took a line a hundred yards or so north of me, within easy shouting distance. I stepped far enough from the boat before I began casting. Our approach was to blind cast, and yet scan the water for any visible signs of trout — the black tip of the tail sticking out of the water; signs of feeding; and nervous water or wakes. The showers ceased, and the sun rose in the east. I still had my jacket on and was getting warm, but I didn't want to stop to take it off. In the distance I heard the cackling and squawking of gulls, terns, and stilts as they commenced their morning reverie. I refrained from glancing in their direction. I wanted to keep my focus. I set the frequency of my mind to sight big trout, ruling out the redfish that might be milling about the flat for their morning fare.

Both Scott and I headed east, slowly wading and scanning the surface for any sign of Grandmother Trout. I blind cast occasionally, not wanting to make my presence known. I wanted the fish to come closer. Except for the three we saw when we got off the boat, I saw no evidence of others. We had a northwest wind — again. It seemed that the "cold" fronts, no matter how mild, would never stop. It was now June, and we'd already had two, a phenomenon that does affect the fish's behavior and predictability. At one point I glanced toward Scott. He was heading for the channel. I opted to follow suit, since the flat seemed devoid of any species worthy of my attention. In the western sky, a muted section of a rainbow caught my eye. I glanced at it occasionally as I cast and waded toward the channel, careful to watch my step. Some time ago, I became so engrossed in my mission that I almost stepped off into the channel. I didn't really feel like going swimming. Between casts, I checked the surface all around me; there were no visible signs of fish. I also watched the rainbow transform into a vibrant swatch of color as the sky behind it darkened. I stayed along the edge for a half hour or so. It was hard to keep track of time on the Bay. It seemed so irrelevant to measure our efforts by minutes. It disrupted the flow and the attunement to nature. I continued alternately casting into the channel and backcast onto the flat.

Suddenly I felt prompted to move. I turned and headed to the east again. *Grandmother Trout, where are you? Bless me with your presence.* A trickling of energy washed over me. *I wonder...* refusing to let myself continue my thought. I moved back to the flat, about 30 yards from the channel. I began enjoying my casting, really allowing my body to dance with the rod. For a moment I forgot my quest. It was so pleasurable just to move with my rod, as if we were one in the same. I got out of my head, and I let go of my intense attachment to locating fish. At one point I let a beautiful cast glide through the air, my fly landing with finesse. A boat zoomed by on the channel, and I heard the familiar phrase: "That's a lady and she's fly fishing." I promptly hooked up. I smiled to myself. *And she can catch fish!* A healthy dose of proper ego is called for occasionally. It's good for the soul. It was a trout. It jumped and dashed around at the end of the line, but before long I reeled it in. I spoke to it sweetly as I freed it from the hook. It measured 16 inches. A beautiful fish, a fine catch. It had been six months since I last hooked up on a trout on the flats, just shortly after Christmas. There had been other fish, but not my most formidable teacher. *Perhaps the ice was thawing. Perhaps my efforts were bearing fruit. Perhaps I had paid my dues.* I thanked him for gracing me with his presence and sent him on his way.

I took a deep breath, and glanced around for telltale signs of his family members. Instantly, I became aware of energy surging through my body, like an electrical current, as if I stuck my finger into an electrical socket. I started to fight it, wondering if it was some how associated with perimenopause. I had been reading that women's bodies go through so many changes in our forties that we are often uncomfortable with the unfamiliar sensations. I looked over at the eastern sky, with my thoughts about my body and my age filtering through my mind. My 44th birthday was just a couple of months away.

The sun was now high over Green Island, illuminating the clouds. It was a beautiful sight. It seemed to symbolize the dawning of a new era for me. I was ready. I no longer feared growing into my cronehood, my wisdom. Wasn't that after all what Grandmother Trout represented? Only the female of the spotted trout species grow over 20 inches. Only they have the wisdom and the capability to perpetuate their kind in a way that their younger sisters cannot. Only the wise women of our species can convey true wisdom to the younger women in our society. I consciously surrendered to the sensations still pulsing beneath my skin, accepting them and any changes that would come in this new stage of my life. Many spiritual teachers believe resistance to change is only the ego's attempt to control our life according to our limiting beliefs about how our life "should" be. I truly wanted to move beyond my self-imposed limitations.

As Ezra Bayda reminds us in *Being Zen*, "resistence...simply perpetuates our pain." I knew my midlife transition would be peaceful only if I surrendered to the process. Most of the time I was enjoying my newly found freedom. It was exciting. It was only during the most stressful periods of my life that the physical shifts were intrusive, and I feared aging to the point where I was no longer fertile.

The energy shifted and I became comfortable again. I wondered if it was something other than a midlife moment. As I turned my head slowly from east to west, something caught my eye. I whirled my head in its direction. A dark tail was sticking out of the water, and it wasn't small. I lifted my rod, and cast. I can't even remember if I made a false cast. I was present and yet I wasn't. There was magic in the air. Something was definitely happening, and yet I couldn't take time to witness it fully. I had an opportunity within my grasp and I wanted to execute it completely. My VIP landed with perfection. I stripped the fly twice. The popper grabbed the fish's attention, just as planned. The fish came up and took the fly with confidence. I was hooked up. I raised my rod. *Did I set the hook? God I hope so.* She thrashed and she ran with determination toward the channel, like a torpedo. *What kind of fish is this?* It wasn't a redfish; there was a subtle difference. For a moment I thought it was a ladyfish. But it had such authority. Ladyfish provide good play, but not like this. It had to be a trout. It was hard to believe, even though I saw the tail, and knew upon casting that it had to be a big trout. *I got her. Yes!* I yelled to Scott. "It's her." I knew by the feel of her on my rod that she was most likely a record. I tried not to dwell on that thought as got all the line onto the reel, something extremely necessary if I was to complete this mission. I did not want any slack in the water this time, not like my encounter with her in December. Then she stopped running and my rod bent, almost in half or so it seemed. There was no movement, just constant pressure. I knew I had a fish on the line, and yet I thought perhaps that my line was caught on something. But, there was nothing to be caught on — no twigs, no branches. This wasn't a freshwater fishery. And I knew there weren't any underwater obstacles here. I'd waded the area so many times, that I knew the bottom intimately. It was semi-soft, with a grassy bottom. She had buried herself in the grass and was determined not to budge. I slowly increased the tension, exerting my authority. Then she darted straight toward me. *Not again!* I'd been played like that before. I frantically reeled in the slack. She was between my legs, and proceeding to wrap herself around my left leg. I lifted my rod high and brought up the remaining slack. *You're not going to do this to me!*

Big trout will use anything they can, any form of structure, in which to break off. I lifted my leg. I freed myself from her clutches. I was still ahead of the game. I made one last daring move to keep her from wrapping herself completely around my right leg. I grabbed the line. I knew that act could go either way, but I was desperate. I could rein her in, or I could break her off. My heart was beating rapidly, and I felt like I was in a race against time. It worked. She lay subdued between my feet. I reached down and grabbed her by the back of the head, my small hand barely able to grasp her securely.

"Do you have a stringer?" Scott asked. He was coming toward me. This must be different. He gave up his own fishing to come assist me.

"Yeah," I replied. I reached around to my pack. My reel was dipping in the water with each move. I didn't care. I'd clean it later. I talked to the fish.

"Listen, no dying on me. That's not allowed." I pulled the stringer out and began untangling it. Even though I hated to hurt the fish, I had to get it off the fly and onto the stringer. I struggled with it. My attempts to puncture its mouth were half-hearted. I hated inflicting pain. But I knew that she agreed be here for me this morning. I surrendered to do my part, and the stringer went in.

Scott took her from me and tied her to his Strip 'n Aid, and buried it deep in the mud. We didn't want to drag her around, creating more stress for the fish that could jeopardize her life. Yet, he had to go back to get the boat in order for her to be weighed and measured. "Keep fishing," he said as he walked away.

I did cast a few times, but not with any real commitment to the process for a variety of reasons. I was shaking all over from the excitement. In addition to wanting to relish the victory, I also feared that another fish might break off my tippet and I'd have nothing to submit to the International Game Fish Association. Scott came up on the boat and we put the fish on the Boga Grip, a hand-held scale, which we had certified by IGFA back in December. She weighed just shy of three pounds, that meant I most likely broke the current record by nearly one pound for the 12-pound tippet record. IGFA determines fly rod world records according to tippet strength. For this class, it meant that my tippet had to withstand up to 12 pounds of pressure without breaking. I was starting to believe this was all a dream. I held the trout in the water, while Scott prepared to measure her on the deck of the boat. She was doing fine and I moved her gently back and forth to keep the water flowing through her gills. Placing her on the deck of the boat, Scott measured her to be just 21 inches. We didn't pinch her tail, which might have added some length. She was wide in the girth for such a "short" fish; rather matronly I'd say. He took her picture and then handed her back to me. I was leaning against the edge of the boat, with her in the water. I looked around hoping to see someone close enough to witness this event. An elderly couple, who I often saw boat by the house in the morning, were fishing nearby. They took off just as I was about to wave them over.

"Scott, I think we better wave a boat down. We really need a witness."

Just at that moment, a boat crossed the northern most end of the Trout Bar. It was a Pathfinder. Scott and I looked at each other. Several people we knew owned this model of boat.

"Hey, that's Dave," Scott said. Dave was a client. He looked our way and I waved him over. He boated to the edge of the channel, and Scott walked out to greet him, pulling his boat over to ours. When they came within earshot, I heard him say, "Congratulations." He then agreed to pose with the fish and me, and to witness the weighing and measuring. With the formalities out of the way, the trout was released. She was "green," meaning that she was full of life. She darted off without looking back.

My mind whirled in amazement at the morning's events. Everything played out perfectly, from having enough gas to get to the Trout Bar — and home again — to a witness appearing just when we needed one. Ask and ye shall receive.

I now have a women's IGFA world fly rod record. Just more evidence of God's grace working in our lives once again.

Kathy releasing her record-breaking trout

Epilogue

I realize that the longing to fish and the longing for stillness is the same. It's the union with God and God's creations that call to me. It makes me ache in a way that can't be noticed by the untrained eye. But I know. This longing can't be lulled into acquiescence by a long nap, a good movie, or a glass of red wine.

Those moments between casts, when the fly gracefully glides through the air. Those moments between breaths, between thoughts. Those moments between fish caught and released. Those moments between visions and inspirations. Those are the moments where I come closer to knowing my Self. Big "S." The times when my self, little "s", is but a mere memory.

I think we're all searching for the same thing — whether we fish, ski, surf, hike, garden, write, or meditate.

It's the union with our true Selves, the part of us that is one with the Divine, that drives us both outward and inward. It is in the practice, the doing — whether we're casting, chanting, or flowing in our asanas — where we are able to perceive perfection and achieve the mastery. However, the road to mastery is long, and everchanging. To reach our goals, and come to know something of our Selves, we need a firm commitment to the journey, a willingness to sit in stillness, observing the breath going in and out. We need to surrender to the movement of the cast, and in doing so perfect our presentations.

With our lines tight, and our rods bent, we come closer to knowing God, and acknowledging our Creator's presence not only within ourselves, but in our fellow anglers, and those delightful creatures that agree to dance with us on the end of our lines.

This part of my journey has come to an end, but before I head back to the water to wet my line, I leave you with this bit of wisdom to ponder in your mind and heart — both on the water and off.

May your rods be bent, and your lines be tight. Dance with those fish, and remember the words of Sparse Gray Hackle, the author of *Fishless Days and Angling Nights:* "Sometimes I think that the least important thing about fishing is catching fish."

Bibliography

Books

Baptiste, Baron. *Journey Into Power: How to Sculpt Your Ideal Body, Free Your True Self, and Transform Your Life with Yoga.* New York: Fireside, 2002.

Bayda, Ezra. *Being Zen.* Boston: Shambhala Publications, 2002.

Belitz, Charlene, and Lundstrom, Meg. *The Power of Flow: Practical Ways to Transform Your Life with Meaningful Coincidence.* New York: Harmony Books, 1997.

Borysenko, Joan, Ph.D. *A Woman's Book of Life: The Biology, Psychology, and Spirituality of the Feminine Life Cycle.* New York: Riverhead Books, 1996.

Breathnach, Sarah Ban. *Simple Abundance: A Daybook of Comfort and Joy.* New York: Warner Books, 1995.

Britton, Joseph C., and Morton, Brian. *Shore Ecology of the Gulf of Mexico.* Austin: University of Texas Press, 1989.

Chidvilasananda, Gurumayi. *Courage and Contentment: A Collection of Talks on Spiritual Life.* South Fallsburg. SYDA Foundation, 1999.

Chidvilasananda, Gurumayi. *Kindle My Heart: Volumes I & II* South Fallsburg: SYDA Foundation, 1989.

Everitt, James H., and Drawe, Lynn D. *Trees, Shrubs & Cacti of South Texas.* Lubbock: Texas Tech University Press, 1993

Foggia, Lyla. Reel Women: *The World of Women Who Fish.* Hillsboro: Beyond Words Publishing, 1995.

Friedman, Bonnie. *Writing Past Dark: Envy, Fear, Distraction and Other Dilemmas — in the Writer's Life*. New York: HarperPerennial, 1994.

Gammel, Bill, and Gammel, Jay. *The Essentials of Fly Casting*. Bozeman: Federation of Fly Fishers, 1993.

Gebhardt, Kris. *Body Mastery*. Indianapolis: Sideline Sports Publishing, 1997.

Hendricks, Gay, Ph.D. *Conscious Breathing: Breathwork for Health, Stress Release, and Personal Mastery*. New York: Bantam, 1995.

Johnson, Robert A., and Ruhl, Jerry Michael. *Balancing Heaven and Earth: A Memoir*. New York: Harper Collins Publishers, 1998.

Khalsa, Dharma Singh, M.D., and Stauth, Cameron. *Meditation as Medicine: Activate the Power of Your Natural Healing Force*. New York: Pocket Books, 2001.

Kornfield, Jack. *A Path with Heart. A Guide through the Perils and Promises of Spiritual Life*. New York: Bantam Doubleday Dell, 1993.

Leonard, Linda Schierse, Ph.D. *Creation's Heartbeat: Following the Reindeer Spirit*. New York: Bantam, 1995.

Leonard, Linda Schierse, Ph.D. *Meeting the Madwoman: Empowering the Feminine Spirit*. New York: Bantam, 1994.

Linn, Denise. *Sacred Legacies: Healing Your Past and Creating a Positive Future*. New York: Ballentine Wellspring, 1999.

Louden, Jennifer. *The Woman's Comfort Book: A Self-Nurturing Guide for Restoring Balance in Your Life*. New York: HarperSanFrancisco, 1992.

Maclean, Norman. *A River Runs Through It and Other Stories*. Chicago: The University of Chicago Press, 1976.

Maxwell, Jessica. *I Don't Know Why I Swallowed the Fly: My Fly Fishing Rookie Season*. Seattle: Sasquatch Books, 1997.

Rama, Swami, Ballentine, Rudolph, M.D., Hymes, Alan, M.D. *Science of Breath: A Practical Guide.* Honesdale: The Himalayan Institute Press, 1998.

Sergeant, Winthrop. *Shri Bhagavad Gita.* Albany: State University of New York Press, 1993.

Sparrow, G. Scott, Ed.D. *Sacred Encounters with Jesus.* Allen: Thomas More, 2002.

Sparrow, G. Scott, Ed.D. *Sacred Encounters with Mary.* Allen: Thomas More, 2001.

Thoreau, Henry David. *Walden.* New York: Quality Paperback Book Club, 1997.

Vanzant, Iyanla. *Faith in the Valley: Lessons for Women on the Journey to Peace.* New York: Fireside, 1996.

Wulff, Joan. *Joan Wulff's Fly Fishing: Expert Advice from a Woman's Perspective.* Harrisburg: Stackpole Books, 1991.

Yogananda, Paramahansa. *Autobiography of a Yogi.* Los Angeles: Self-Realization Fellowship, 1990.

Zhorne, Jeff. *The Everything Fly-Fishing Book: From casting to catching and everything in between, the art and science of America's most idyllic sport.* Holbrook: Adams Media Corporation, 1999.

Magazines

Catalfo, Phil. "The 2001 Karma Yoga Awards." *Yoga Journal,* (December 2001). 83.

Gay, Phil. "Teaching Casting Mechanics On-Stream." *The Loop,* (Spring 2002). 2.

Sparrow, Scott. "Texas Trout: Welcome to My Passion — How to Get Big Speckled Trout to take a Fly." *Fish and Fly,* (Spring 2002). 32-38.

Tigunait, Pandit Rajmani. "The Doorway to the Future." *Yoga International,* (February/March 1999). 38-44.

Audiotape

Gurumayi Chidvilasananda's Message for 2001. *Approach the present with your heart's consent, Make it a blessed event.* South Fallsburg: SYDA Foundation, 2001.

Video

Coastal Fly Fishing with Ken Hanley & Friends. Fremont: Pill Enterprises and Adventures Beyond, 2001.

About the Author

Kathy Sparrow is an award-winning writer, and one of the only female saltwater fly fishing guides in the country. She writes and speaks on the topics of fly fishing, women's issues, creative writing, and spirituality.

A veteran of the publishing industry for nearly 20 years, Kathy has recently completed a screenplay based on her husband's book, *Andrew's Quest for Perfect Gift*, which is currently under option by Pill Enterprises.

Her work has appeared in national and regional publications, such as *E Magazine, American Fitness, Indiana Business Magazine, Hudson Valley Magazine, Hartford Monthly, Venture Inward*, and *Indianapolis Woman*. She is a contributing writer to *Indianapolis: Crossroads of the American Dream* (Towery Publishing, Inc. 1996).

Her interests include fly fishing, yoga, spiritual studies, heritage birding, and native plant landscaping. She is married to psychotherapist, fly-fishing guide, and author G. Scott Sparrow, and their blended family includes three children — Shana, Pete, and Ryan.

The Sparrows own Kingfisher Inn, a fly fishing lodge in Arroyo City, Texas, where they share the magic of the Lower Laguna Madre with fly fishers, birders, and nature-enthusiasts.

Kathy feels that her mission is to encourage others to make positive changes in their lives. Realizing that she can become a beacon only by example, she has dedicated her life to personal and spiritual growth, and sharing her journey with others.

She is currently working on her second novel.